THE SOURCE OF SMOKE

THE SOURCE OF SMOKE

V. L. ADAMS

NEW DEGREE PRESS

THE SOURCE OF SMOKE

ISBN   979-8-88504-147-8   *Paperback*

979-8-88504-779-1   *Kindle Ebook*

979-8-88504-258-1   *Ebook*

For Nate,
You know why.

CONTENTS

CHAPTER 1

Charlie Allen slammed her palm against the metal door of the mailbox with enough force to leave her hand smarting and the sound echoing in the air.

It wasn't the mailbox's fault, but she needed an outlet for her anger. The mailbox happened to be an easy target. It wasn't the mailman's fault either, but she was a little bitter at him right now as well.

Charlie stomped up the stairs and flung open the heavy oak front door to the blue-and-white craftsman home her nana had left her. Before the door had a chance to slam behind her, she was immediately greeted by her black lab, Buck. He licked her hand and nuzzled her leg through her ripped jeans as if he could sense that she needed comfort. She stopped to scratch his ears while she tried to calm herself.

Breathe, Charlie. Deep breath in... deep breath out... in... out.

The smell of the kale mac and cheese she made earlier that day mixed with the aromas of the house to form a slightly stale smell with hints of potpourri and beechnut left over from her grandparents. She felt her throat constrict and she wished for the days when Nana could kiss her forehead and make the bad stuff disappear.

Focusing on her breath had calmed her slightly. But a glance at the letter in her hand had her heart racing again. Getting the mail hadn't started it. Charlie had been uptight and fidgety all day. All week, actually.

A week ago, she'd started having a hard time sleeping. She thought if she exercised enough during the day, she would pass out at night. But each night she fell in bed, only to watch the blades of the fan until the early morning hours. She woke up tangled in sheets and more exhausted than when she'd lain down.

She hadn't been able to concentrate or sit still either, so instead of working, she spent most of her time pacing. She forgot to eat lunch yesterday, she couldn't taste dinner last night, and her stomach was in knots this morning. She even burned her hand on the kettle while making ginger tea.

It was September 30. The anniversary of her sister Dani's death—the worst day of the year.

The day marked the loss of Charlie's favorite person. It was also the day when Charlie left the life of independence she'd chosen for herself in Dallas. She gave it up for a life living in her grandmother's house in the eastern Oklahoma town she thought she had left for good to raise someone else's child. While Charlie would freely admit that raising Rainna was the best part of her life, it didn't change the fact she wasn't the one who was supposed to have that job.

But as horrible as it was for Charlie to remember everything that happened on that day three years ago, it wasn't the reason she couldn't sleep, forgot to eat, and hit mailboxes.

It had all started with a letter—one that arrived in the recently abused mailbox precisely two years ago. On the first anniversary of Dani's death, Charlie had heard the metal door of the mailbox squeak shut, letting her know that the postman had made his delivery. With a handful of letters, she started walking back up the sidewalk to her front steps. That's when she saw it underneath a solicitation for car insurance. The unassuming white envelope bore a stamp from the state penitentiary.

Charlie only knew of one person who might send her mail from prison—the man convicted of killing her sister. And he was the last person she wanted a letter from.

She didn't open it. She didn't want to. And no one could make her.

On her way through the kitchen to the trash can, she stopped and looked at the letter. As much as she wanted to, she didn't think she could throw it away. She jerked open the messy drawer filled with unused appliance manuals and shoved the letter haphazardly into the mess. She tried to slam the drawer, only to have it go in sideways and get stuck. After emptying the drawer, realigning it, and then refilling it, she was finally able to walk away.

Looking back, she was surprised at how easily she'd forgotten that first letter. "Out of sight, out of mind" could be true, especially when Charlie spent most of her time adjusting to parenthood and chasing a toddler.

On the second anniversary, she felt a tiny prickle of apprehension when she went to get the mail. Still, she managed to convince herself she was being paranoid. He would probably only send a letter one time, on the first anniversary, and she would never see anything from him again. She had stepped off the broken cement curb and into the street, chanting under her breath. "Please be empty. Please be empty." When she stuck her hand in the mailbox, she knew that she was wrong. Only one envelope sat in the box; a standard white letter-size envelope with the stamp marking its origination as the state penitentiary.

She'd gone inside, found the first letter and stood over the trash. In one motion, both letters could be gone, but she couldn't do it. So she stuck them in the drawer, slamming it shut. Once again, the old drawer got out of line, and she had to spend time fixing it instead of ditching the letter and escaping the memories they brought up.

After the second anniversary, she couldn't put the letters out of her mind, even when they were out of her sight. Over the last year, she'd gone to the drawer about fifty times trying to draw up enough courage to see what he had to say. Somehow she always found a way of talking herself out of it. She would let go of the cold metal drawer pull and tiptoe away, pretending she had never been there.

Today, however, Charlie could no longer fool herself into thinking she wouldn't receive another letter. She wasn't sure how he could time his mail so well—she couldn't even get a letter across town in a timely manner, and she wasn't in prison—but she knew what she would find. As she opened the mailbox, she saw it in the middle of a stack of junk mail and bills, a perfectly ordinary envelope with a prison stamp. Once again, the man who killed her sister had written her. Three letters for three years.

Maybe he wanted to apologize. Perhaps he was evil and wanted to taunt Charlie. Maybe it was something else entirely. It didn't matter what he wanted. What mattered to Charlie was that she wanted to get rid of the dread and stop feeling like a coward. She still remembered the look in his dark eyes when he took the witness stand and told the courtroom, "I'm innocent."

She walked through the front door with purpose. Charlie went straight to the drawer with the other two letters. She dug them out of the mess of manuals and laid all three on the dining room table. Looking up, she stared at her reflection in the mirror hanging over the table.

I'm doing this. No more stalling, no more letting him make me a coward.

She met her hazel eyes in the mirror, pushed her long dark hair behind her ears, and straightened her thin frame to pull herself to her full height.

Charlie picked up the three letters and examined the postage stamps. She placed the two more recent letters on the 1920s dark wood dining table and examined the first. She hesitantly ran her finger over her neatly printed name and address. Sticking her index finger in the opening of the letter, she attempted to pull the adhesive apart but ended up ripping it open and making a mess of the envelope. Inside was a single piece of paper, folded into thirds to fit neatly.

The script was precise and not the scratchy, slanted, almost illegible handwriting that she had been used to seeing from her former law school classmates.

Charlie,

I know I'm the last person you want to hear from, and I hate the idea of causing you more pain than what you've already gone through. You have no reason to believe me, but I did—

A high-pitched repetitive sound bounced around the room, grating on Charlie's nerves and leaving her ears ringing. The page fell from her fingers as she scrambled to shut off the alarm on her phone. *Crap!* Her alarm meant that she was late to pick up her niece, Rainna, from preschool.

Charlie learned the hard way to always have a backup plan. Shortly after Dani died, Charlie had lost track of time while setting up the layout for a sponsored post on her food blog. The daycare called when Charlie hadn't shown up and they were trying to close. It shouldn't have been a big deal, parents run late all the time, but one of the teachers at the school had gossiped about it. The incident took place right before Rainna's custody hearing, and Charlie's dad and cousin—who both wanted custody—tried to say that because Charlie had forgotten to pick Rainna up a single day, she wasn't fit to be guardian. Luckily, the judge honored Dani's wishes from her last will and testament and Charlie got custody.

Since then, she'd kept an alarm on her phone to warn her when it was time to pick up Rainna. She didn't need to give the town any more reason to gossip about her.

Charlie grabbed her keys off the hook and pulled the front door shut. She swore under her breath as she pushed and pulled on the handle to get the deadbolt to line up with the strike plate on the frame so she could lock it. After a few tries, she got the door secured and headed to her Jeep.

Several cars were still in the parking lot and kids in the building when Charlie arrived. She had made it in time to avoid any aunt-shaming from the moms and teachers.

"Auntie!" Rainna screamed when she saw Charlie.

It never ceased to amaze Charlie the joy she felt every time Rainna greeted her. Rainna was the type of kid whose happiness seeped out of her pores. When she was in a good mood, her body wiggled, and she did a little dance like she had to find an outlet for her emotions.

Rainna wore hot pink leggings and a polka dot shirt that reflected her boisterous personality and contrasted sharply against Charlie's usual outfit of a neutral cotton top and jeans. Charlie bent down in time to catch Rainna in a massive hug as Rainna ran straight for her. The smell of sweaty child, outside, and watermelon hit her like a brick.

"Did you get another sucker from Ms. Neelan?" she asked Rainna, looking down with a mock stern expression.

"I'm not telling!" Rainna responded while crossing her arms and trying to mimic her aunt. The curls in her long black hair were in knots and she was squinting her brown eyes.

"I bet I can get you to tell," Charlie teased as she reached toward Rainna's ribcage and started tickling.

Rainna dissolved into a fit of giggles. "Stop! Okay, okay, I give! Stop, Auntie!" she begged, breathing hard and still laughing. "Yes! I had a bubble pop!" she admitted.

Charlie always melted a little when Rainna used her particular phrase for a sucker. "Well, I hope you did more than just eat candy today." Charlie winked at Rainna. "Alright, sweets! Let's head out. I have a special dinner prepped."

"Mac and cheese?" Rainna asked, always hoping for one of her favorites.

Charlie bent down so that her face was on Rainna's level and tried to make her voice sound tough. "You want mac and cheese? I made you fancy salmon yesterday, and you ask for boring old mac and cheese?" Rainna giggled. "Fine. I guess you can have mac and cheese, but you know my rule." The two of them continued together, "If you don't add a little spice, you're not doing it right."

Charlie buckled Rainna into her car seat, trying to ignore the drink stains and stray Cheerios. She didn't mind a little mess, but she was always blown away by how disgusting kids could get things in practically no time at all.

After a quick drive listening to nursery rhyme songs, she and Rainna raced up the stairs and into the house.

Charlie pulled out her grandmother's cornflower CorningWare casserole dish from the refrigerator. It was filled with the prepped mac and cheese that she had put together earlier in the day. She had worked on the recipe for a while and thought it was finally ready for her blog. Charlie had taken the prep photos as she put together the ingredients. She would take a few shots of the dish in the oven and after she finished baking it. Rainna loved to help with the pictures of the finished product by taking a utensil and scooping out a huge bite. But Rainna's chubby hand holding a spoon or a fork was all that ever appeared in a post photo. Charlie was protective of their privacy.

Her food blog started out more as a journal and evolved into a full-time job. One of her law school classmates in Austin loved her cooking so much, he'd created a place for her to share the recipes. And then another classmate had submitted her blog as a feature to a legal website that posted stories about lawyers or law students and their side hustles or passions. The legal website posted about Charlie a week after she put up a story about lighting her apartment on fire when using too much liquor in chocolate fondue. It struck a chord with people, and her followers blew up overnight. She enjoyed the creativity and writing so much that when she and her ex split up after her second year of law school, she decided to pursue it full time, rather than finish her degree. Now, several years later it still paid the bills.

She had only gone to law school because a guy in undergrad had bet a bunch of his friends that none of them could make a higher score on the LSAT than he could. If any of them did, he said he'd give them a thousand dollars. Charlie always liked a challenge, so she took the test and scored four points higher. She got the money, and he talked her into a date, then into applying for law school, and finally into marrying him. But Charlie quickly discovered that he wanted her to be something she wasn't—polished, professional, and a lawyer's perfect wife. Charlie preferred to be messy, creative, and independent.

"It smells so cheesy in here, Auntie!" Rainna said, practically bouncing on the balls of her feet in excitement. Buck was right beside Rainna, hoping for a bite of whatever they dropped. "Wait! Why is it green? Did you put salad in it?" she asked, her eyebrows scrunched and her lips pursed, all excitement from moments before quickly dissolving as she saw the casserole dish full of pasta coated in a green cheese sauce.

Charlie wanted to laugh at how adorable Rainna was when something didn't meet her expectations.

"Okay, okay. Calm down. It's not salad, silly girl. Let's take these pics, and then you can make your mind up if you like it. If not, you can have chicken nuggets." Charlie had blended kale into the sauce, making the dish green, but the white cheddar was strong enough to cover the kale flavor. Rainna was going to love it.

Rainna held her nose to avoid the "salad" smell and put a small bite into her mouth for the first taste. Charlie sat back, trying to keep the smile off her face. Rainna's expression started out looking like she was pained. Then it shifted to thoughtful, and finally, it changed to approving. "It's not that bad," she said as she ate another bite. Charlie was laughing by the time Rainna shoveled the last spoonful in her mouth. "We can have this again, Auntie."

After dinner, Rainna played with her dolls while Charlie cleaned up the kitchen. "Five more minutes," Charlie called out, letting Rainna know she would be going to bed soon.

"What's this paper, Auntie? It's got my name on it!" Rainna walked into the room holding the letter that had caused so much anxiety in Charlie hours before.

CHAPTER 2

Seeing the paper in Rainna's little hand brought the events of earlier in the day back to Charlie like a shock of static. She had left the letters in the formal dining room, which also served as a storage area for Rainna's toys. At four and a half, Rainna was learning to read and could pick out her name and a few other words.

The past two hours had been a fun and silly blur filled with laughter and cheesy goodness, but suddenly the cheese and pasta felt too heavy in her stomach.

"Well," she started, feeling her voice shake. "It's a letter to me from someone who knew your mommy."

Charlie had a strict "no lying" rule when raising Rainna, but that didn't mean she told her everything. Death was a complicated concept for a child that young, and as much as she tried to be open, she still some hadn't figured out how to share some things.

"A letter from mommy's friend? Will you read it to me?"

Rainna wiggled around like she couldn't stay still at the prospect of a letter from someone who knew her mommy. She was obsessed with anything to do with her mom, and

Charlie should have known that she would latch on and want to learn more. She bent down to Rainna's level and looked at the wide, brown eyes that looked so much like Dani's. Charlie took a deep breath to steady her nerves and muster her courage, "I haven't read it yet, sweets. Let me read it first. It might be a letter just for grown-ups. But if I think it's okay, one day I'll read it to you or let you read it yourself."

Rainna crossed her arms, and her face scrunched up the same way it had when she'd seen the mac and cheese was green. "No fair. Why do grown-ups always get to decide? I'm a big girl, and it's got my name!"

Charlie knelt to pull Rainna to her for a hug. Rainna tried to resist but finally let her body sink into Charlie's. "I'm sorry, sweets."

Charlie placed the letter back on the table and turned to go to the kitchen. As she was turning, she saw Rainna take the letter back off the table.

"I can read some of this, Auntie. I don't see why you won't read it to me." Charlie's heart sped up, but she reminded herself that Rainna's reading was very limited. Rainna didn't often push her boundaries, but she was still a kid who liked to see what she could get away with. Taking a deep breath, Charlie decided to see what Rainna would do.

After looking through the letter and picking out "I," "the," "you," and "no," Rainna got bored and set the letter back on to the table. She went back to playing with her toys and Charlie finished in the kitchen, breathing a sigh of relief.

A few minutes later, Charlie carried Rainna to bed singing, "Rock-A-Bye Baby," and pretending to drop Rainna when it was time for the cradle to fall. Buck's nails clicked on the stairs as he followed them up for their nightly routine.

They were both laughing as they filled the bathtub with bubbles and water, but Charlie's mind was still on the letter waiting for her on the dining room table.

After her bath, they read two books, an early reader for Rainna to work her way through sounding out words like "cat" and "who," and one book with a colorful pachyderm that Charlie gravitated toward when Rainna let her pick. Charlie then pulled up the unicorn comforter and tucked Rainna in.

"Your mommy would be so proud of you, little one. Just like I am." She felt her throat constrict, and she blinked to control the tears that sprang to her eyes. Rainna grabbed a lock of hair and put it in her mouth.

Figuring out how much and when to tell Raina details about Dani's death was intimidating. She knew from the teachers at school that the other kids had picked up that Rainna's family was different. Father's Day was always awkward. Up until this year, Rainna had been able to make crafts at school for her grandpa. But after his death in the spring, Rainna was left without a male figure in her life. Most of the kids in class called Charlie Rainna's mommy at pick up and drop off. She had never corrected them, but it was still jarring each time Charlie heard it.

"How about I tell you a story about your mommy?" she asked. Rainna nodded her head quickly. She always soaked up stories of her mom like a snake on a rock soaked up the sun.

Charlie told Rainna several short stories about Dani from when they were young, like how Dani never made a peep when she had to get shots at the doctor. She also told her how Dani was always there to wipe Charlie's tears and clean up her scrapes. Dani had known what to do to make others feel better.

Dani had been short and spunky. She had short dark hair, a quick smile, an easy laugh, and copper skin that seemed to glow. She was one of those people who made everyone feel welcome. She loved karaoke, even though she was horrible at it and was obsessed with camels because she thought they were underappreciated. Her job as an ER nurse allowed her to meet and care for new people constantly.

"One time when she was young, your mommy got hurt. She fell on a sharp rock and got a cut on her leg about this big," Charlie held her fingers about two inches apart. "I remember going to the hospital with her. I was little and I was crying the whole time. But your mommy was calm. She held my hand and kept telling me I was going to be okay, even though she was the one who was hurt."

"Whoa," Rainna said. "I wanna be strong like that."

"You are strong, sweets. And you're right. Your mommy was strong," Charlie told Rainna. "Her strength brought you into this world, and I will forever be grateful." Charlie kissed the top of Rainna's head, inhaling the lavender shampoo that made her think of innocence.

"Auntie?" Rainna asked as Charlie moved to turn on the sound machine that played white noise all night. "Why did mommy have to die? Grandpa was old when he died, but Tommy's parents are older than mommy."

Charlie took a shaky breath. She clenched her hands into fists until she could feel her nails digging into her palms. "I don't know," she said in a strained voice. Clearing her throat, she shook her head. "I don't know why your mommy had to die so young. Sometimes people do. And it's not fair." Her voice came out at barely a whisper, and she didn't think she would be able to string any more words together even if she tried.

"I miss my mommy," came the sleepy reply from the bed. Rainna sounded sad and tired, so Charlie gave her one last hug and kiss.

"I know, sweets. Me too." Rainna curled under the covers, and Charlie eased the door shut behind her.

The moment the door shut, she felt the tears. She moved down the hall, away from Rainna's room, and sank with her back against the wall. She rested her head on her knees. *Charlie, you're in way over your head.* She fought the anxiety that threatened to bubble to the surface whenever she thought about all the ways she could screw up. Buck made his way to her and started licking the salty tears from her face, leaving her with a face full of dog breath.

After counting backward from one hundred, Charlie finally felt together enough to move away from the wall. She made her way to the dining room table and retrieved the letter Rainna had found. Charlie also grabbed the other two that were still where she had left them earlier in the day. She took all three with her as she made her way to her grandmother's paisley-patterned wingback chair in the living room. Even from a young age, Charlie had loved to sit in it. Her grandmother had sat there to read all her romance novels, and the chair always felt like a hug from Nana. Charlie couldn't think of a time when she needed one of those hugs more than now.

Without putting it off anymore, Charlie looked at the first letter.

Charlie,

I know I'm the last person you want to hear from, and I hate the idea of causing you more pain than what you've already gone through. You have no reason to believe me, but I did not and would never hurt your sister.

She said you were her favorite person in the world other than Rainna. Dani said that the thing she admired most about you was that you weren't afraid to chart your course—that you don't believe something just because everyone else does. I'm starting to believe everyone will always think I did this. It's important to me that you don't. The person who loved Dani the most should know the truth. I didn't do this. You and Rainna deserve to know who did. I wish I knew who did. I think about it every single day.

What I can tell you is that I had no reason to do it. Dani and I were having fun; we made a good team. We had a great night, and I left her place a little before midnight. I was home before three that morning. There's no way I could have been there when they say she died.

Please think about what you know and what I'm telling you. You sat through the trial. Can you believe I did this "beyond a reasonable doubt"? Don't believe this just because everyone else in your town does. Make up your mind. Don't let them make it for you.

Darius Thomas

Charlie dropped the letter as if she had grabbed a hot pan from the oven without an oven mitt. She shoved her hands in her hair, only to realize she still had a braid in from when she was cooking dinner. Now she had mussed it up. She jumped to her feet and walked a loop through the kitchen, living room, and dining room. She shook out her hands as she walked.

No, no, no. Charlie stopped and sat back down. She put her head in her hands and massaged her temples. *This isn't happening. He did it. Why can't he admit it?*

Charlie's phone buzzed and she reached into her back pocket to see her best friend Winnie was calling. If Charlie didn't answer, Winnie would call back in five minutes. Charlie hit the button to answer and held the phone up to her ear. "Hey, Win."

"Hey, Char. Just wanted to check on you. I know today had to be tough." Charlie could hear water running along with the clink of dishes, and she imagined Winnie standing at the sink cleaning up after dinner. Winnie had the sandy blonde hair and blue eyes that ran in her family, and she wore the curves that accompanied motherhood well. Charlie and Winnie had been friends since kindergarten, and she didn't think she could have made it through losing Dani and learning to be a parent without Winnie's help.

"Do you think he did it?" Charlie blurted. Charlie hadn't told Winnie about the letters, and she wasn't sure she was ready now. But when Winnie's name had flashed across the screen, she realized they'd never talked about Dani's murder or the trial. She thought she knew Winnie's opinion, but maybe it was worth asking.

"What are you talking about?" said Winnie with an amused tone. "What's got you so fired up this time? Start at the beginning."

Charlie and Winnie were opposites in so many ways but had always been supportive of one another. Winnie had never aspired to a life outside their hometown. They fell out of touch for a few years when Charlie was finishing college and starting law school, something that was probably Charlie's fault because she was focused on school and her ex. But when Charlie started blogging, Winnie had reached out to support her. Having Winnie back in her life was invaluable. She was a source of stability for Charlie through the divorce and even more so when Charlie was thrust into parenting unexpectedly.

Winnie hadn't had it easy, either. She'd had her first baby a few years out of high school. Without the dad in the picture, Winnie had to figure out parenthood and a career on her own. She became a court reporter and met a lawyer from a nearby town, who swept her off her feet. Now they had three kids total.

"I know you were in the trial," she said quickly. She didn't need to clarify which one. Winnie would know what she meant. "I'm wondering if anything made you think he didn't do it?"

"Wait, this is about Dani? When you asked if I thought he did it, I thought you were talking about something Ethan did. Honey, what has you worked up?" Winnie asked. The tone mixed in with Winnie's Southern twang made it sound like she thought Charlie had finally lost it.

When Charlie didn't answer, Winnie filled the silence. "Char, you sat through the whole thing. The jury didn't even take a full day to make up their mind. If they had any questions, don't you think it would have taken them a little longer? Sweetie, I can't imagine how hard these past few years have been for you, but you need to move forward. Not backward."

Charlie ran her hand through her hair, only to have it stop on her braid once more. She reached up and yanked the tie out of her hair.

"Winnie," Charlie paused and took a deep breath, "I don't actually remember the trial." Charlie felt the pressure in her chest ease a bit at her confession.

CHAPTER 3

Silence followed on Winnie's end of the line and then a loud thump, like she'd dropped something.

"What?" Winnie whispered. "I mean... what?"

"I know I sat through the trial," Charlie started in a stronger voice. "But I can't remember any of the testimony. I can tell you stupid, random details. I know what I wore each day. And one day my skirt was itchy. Every time the district attorney addressed the jury, spit would fly out of his mouth, making me worry that jurors needed face shields. The judge played with his mustache like Waluigi. The defense attorney had a constantly furrowed brow. Darius bounced his knee almost constantly, and I could see him flexing his hands under the table. I can tell you the details that most people probably never noticed, but I don't remember anything important."

Charlie sat down at one of the dining room chairs and laid her head on her arms. "How do I know if he did it? How do I stop myself from wondering?" she asked.

"It's not your job to question. I know it's what you do, but you're only hurting yourself. The police investigated. The DA made his case. The jury made up their minds. It's over.

Everyone else knows it's over. You need to move on. Your life has been in limbo for the last three years. Snap out of it. I've watched you spend your time thinking about everybody else. It's time to live a little bit for yourself." Winnie sounded like she did when she was giving her kids a lecture and Charlie could imagine her standing in the kitchen with her hands on her hips.

Charlie winced; she hadn't realized Winnie felt that way. "But it all happened so quickly," Charlie said. She was hurt and offended that Winnie had dismissed her concerns. Also, it felt better to argue. "He was arrested so fast. Did they even look at anyone else?"

Being a mom of three had made Winnie simultaneously more understanding and more direct. Those attributes coupled with their history explained why Charlie turned to Winnie when she needed another opinion. But maybe Winnie's judgment was clouded on this issue.

The water shut off on Winnie's end and the clink of dishes stopped. "Charlie, I've never talked to you about this because... well, because we never talk about this stuff. You've never brought up the murder or the trial, so I never wanted to push you. Also, I always kinda assumed you'd heard it from someone else. But if you're feeling like this, maybe you never heard about it." Winnie sighed. "Honey, he confessed."

Charlie sucked in a breath.

"No," she shook her head. "I would have heard about it. They would have used it in the trial. No one who's confessed would ever take the stand and say they're not guilty. It doesn't make sense." Charlie's voice gained a rigid quality as she was talking.

"Charlie, you know I don't get all the legal crap, so I'm probably gonna say this wrong, but there was an issue with the confession—something about the timing of when they read him his rights. The way I heard it, right after they brought him in, Harvey asked Darius if he did it. Harvey swears Darius confessed. The camera in the conference room they were in wasn't working, so they didn't have a recording. When Ethan got there, he read Darius his rights and tried to get him to confess again, but he lawyered up. His lawyer was able to keep the confession out of court," Winnie said sounding annoyed with the legal hurdles.

Charlie rubbed her temples again, trying to wrap her brain around everything she was hearing. It was becoming clear that she had missed some things over the last few years.

"I can tell you're trying to decide whether or not you want to listen to me. So don't. Don't listen to me. Talk to Ethan. You know he would love any opportunity to spend time with you," Winnie said.

Charlie could almost hear her friend winking through the phone. It was impressive how quickly Winnie could go from having a serious conversation to turning the tables and playing matchmaker. One of the things Charlie loved about Winnie was that she didn't take life too seriously, and she always found a way to lighten the mood. But it still rubbed her the wrong way at times like these.

"As chief, he ran the investigation and knows about this stuff better than anyone else," Winnie said.

Ethan was Winnie's older brother and the local police chief. He was also Charlie's ex-boyfriend from high school, who had been trying to get rid of that "ex" in his title ever since she'd moved back to town.

"You're just suggesting that because you want me to go out with Ethan again," Charlie chided. Winnie's suggestion made sense, but it didn't mean she didn't see the scheming going on in Winnie's mind. When Charlie had moved back and Ethan was still single, Winnie convinced herself it was because he was still pining for Charlie. Winnie took it upon herself to thrust Ethan and Charlie together at every opportunity, despite Charlie's requests to stop. Charlie let out the breath that she was holding and tried not to get annoyed at Winnie for not listening.

"Thanks, Win," Charlie said, feeling a little more in control of her emotions than when Winnie had called. "I'll think about talking to Ethan. And, Win, can you please stop with the Charlie and Ethan thing? We've been down that road. We don't want the same things."

"You can be such a stick in the mud," Winnie said. "Fine. If you don't need anything else, I hear the little one crying. I'll talk to you tomorrow. Okay, bye!" Winnie finished in a high-pitched girly voice.

"Okay, bye!" Charlie responded in kind. It was their traditional, silly way to end conversations, and Charlie was used to abrupt ends to their calls due to kids.

Winnie hadn't given Charlie what she was hoping for in the conversation. But then again, Charlie didn't know what she expected when she'd asked Winnie's opinion. It was instinct. She felt lonely and wanted to share the burden, even if she didn't want to share the details. Winnie had given her a lot more to think about and possibly more questions than answers.

Charlie stood, pulled her shoulders back, and walked straight to where she had left the letters. She looked for the date stamp showing which letter was second. A tearing sound split through the quiet house as she ripped open the envelope.

Charlie's hands were unsteady as she unfolded the paper and her heart sped up. She wondered if this letter would be the same as the last.

Charlie,

It's been a year, and I haven't heard from you. Not that I expected to. Either you don't believe me, or you threw the letter straight into the trash. I wouldn't blame you either way.

I'm sure you've heard by now that my appeals failed. After the trainwreck of a trial, I'm not sure why I expected anything different. I fought the best I could. Maybe I never had a chance.

This is destroying my parents. They came to visit a few weeks ago and looked like they had aged ten years. I know it's devastating to my brother, too, but he tries not to let me see. You and I aren't the only ones who've suffered.

You're probably expecting me to make my case. To tell you why I'm innocent. I wish I knew how. I still don't understand how the jury thought there was enough evidence. It seems like the only thing I had against me was my relationship and the fact that a cop pulled me over that night for being Black.

I hope this year has been easier for you. I hope that even if you still believe I'm guilty, you can still see me as a person and not a monster. One day, I hope you'll know that I'm *not the guy who killed Dani and left Rainna without a mother.*

Darius

Charlie let out the breath she hadn't even realized she was holding. Her heart was racing, and she had sweat under her arms and on her palms.

She wanted to stop, but in her head, she could hear a forgetful fish from one of Rainna's favorite movies urging her to keep going. She had spent too much time with Rainna's entertainment if, in her moment of crisis, a cartoon character was giving her a pep talk.

Charlie's right hand reached out and snatched the third letter, making short work of the envelope and leaving it a frayed mess. This time she found two sheets of paper.

Unfolding the pages, her eyes skimmed the small, precise print.

Charlie,

This sucks. I don't even know why I'm writing you anymore. I just want someone other than my family to know the truth. But to be honest, I'm on the edge of losing hope that will ever happen. Every day is lonely and hopeless. I am surrounded by murderers and rapists who think I'm one of them. Can you imagine what it's like to be surrounded by people who think you raped and killed your girlfriend?

I've given up on the system, but I haven't given up on myself. I tutor some of the younger guys to keep from endless days of self-pity. I've even taken anger management and victim impact courses to pass the time. But it's hard when I never had a problem with anger until I got here, and being here is what makes me angry.

It would be crazy for me to ask for you to believe me if I were guilty. But if I did it, wouldn't there have been more evidence? Yes, my DNA was on your sister. We were in a relationship, and I admitted we had a date that night.

Can you think of anyone else who could have hurt Dani? I'm not pointing fingers, but I can think of at least two people who the police should have looked into more: that jerk of a doctor who was her ex and the patient who was convinced he was Rainna's father. Maybe the police did look. But it seemed like they zeroed in on me pretty damn fast.

The cops and the DA saw what they wanted to see. It's easy to assume that the boyfriend did it. Especially when I wasn't local, and I'm Black when the town's not.

I've been reading through my trial transcripts, and something caught my attention. Dani said you spent two years at law school, so I'm sure you understand this sort of thing better than I do. I could talk to my lawyer about it, but my case isn't urgent since I'm not on death row. But then again, it might not be anything.

Did the system fail me because I somehow failed her? I should have stayed that night. If I had, she wouldn't have been alone to face whoever showed up. I didn't have anything to do with the head injury, but were the candles we lit that night somehow responsible for the fire?

I don't have a right to, but I'm asking you to believe me. I'm asking you to take a chance. To think about talking to me. To consider that maybe they got it wrong. If you're asking why you, it's simple. There's no one else. You were the one who pressured the DA and made sure he didn't go for the death penalty. You get the law. You know the players and they know you. And whether you like it or not, you're an outsider, like me.

If you don't want to talk to me, consider talking to my brother. Malachi knows me better than anyone. While he's incredibly loyal, he also has a solid moral compass. If Chi thought there was a possibility I did this, he would leave me here to pay for my sins. Maybe you could ask him why he thinks I didn't do it.

I hope these letters aren't going in the trash unread. I hope you care about making sure the person who really killed Dani pays. I hope you're not the kind of person who is okay with someone innocent being in prison. And I hope you're brave enough to do something.

Darius

Charlie's hands were shaking as she set the letter back on the table.

Opening the first letter was like opening Pandora's box. If her pounding head and aching stomach were indications, she wasn't going to be able to let this go. She couldn't now; she had too many questions. It was no longer an option for her to keep her head down and focus on her own life. Charlie had learned too much tonight to pretend like this never happened.

She had some choices to make. Should she reach out to Malachi? Get the transcript? Talk to Ethan? Talk to Darius? She didn't want to go down this rabbit hole, but maybe she never had a choice.

CHAPTER 4

———

Charlie hadn't fallen asleep until around three in the morning, and when she woke her eyes itched like she had run through a field of ragweed.

She made toast and tea to settle her stomach, but the churning sensation remained. After dropping Rainna off at school, she returned home to get some work done.

After an hour of not accomplishing anything, Charlie grabbed the keys and started driving. She had tried to write up the text for her blog post but gave up when she looked down at her computer screen and read, "add pasta to boiling water pasta to boiling water pasta."

She drove on autopilot and ended up parked outside the courthouse. As she chewed her thumbnail, she stared at the yellow brick building built in the twenties. The courthouse was a three-story, rectangular building that housed the courtrooms, government offices, and the court clerk's office. Next to the courthouse was a smaller, matching building with the police and the local jail.

She drummed her fingers on the steering wheel as she weighed her options. *Transcript or Ethan? Neither? Keep driving?*

A loud tap at the passenger window snapped her out of her thoughts.

"Yoo-hoo! Charlie! What are you doing? Get out of your car this minute and give me a hug! And stop chewing on your nails, girl!"

Charlie's older cousin Betti was just visible through the bottom of the passenger window. Betti was only a little over five feet tall, and the Jeep's windows were a stretch for her. But the chunky highlights on her dark brown hair were distinctive, and Charlie could recognize her by only the top of her head. Betti was a nail technician and always gave Charlie a hard time for not taking better care of her nails.

Charlie hopped out of the Jeep and was enveloped in a warm hug that smelled like vanilla lotion. Betti's curvy frame was wrapped in a bright yellow floral kimono and skinny jeans, and her head rested under Charlie's chin during the embrace. The warmth of the hug had Charlie racking her brain for the last time she had been hugged by someone other than a child.

"Where's that sweet baby of mine? Is she at school?" Betti asked, peeking into Charlie's back seat. "I still don't know how you manage to send her away all day. I wouldn't be able to do it. But you already know that—with me keeping all four of my boys at home until they started kindergarten."

Charlie clenched her jaw when she heard Betti call Rainna "her baby." Charlie knew it probably seemed like a term of endearment to outsiders, but Betti meant it literally.

When Charlie's sister turned thirty, she told Charlie she wouldn't wait any longer for a baby. Dani quickly went through the steps to get a sperm donor and was pregnant in a few months.

She miscarried. Not long after that, Dani discovered she had a rare form of cancer caused by the placenta from her miscarriage turning into a mass of cysts. Charlie and Dani's mother had died of cancer when they were younger, so the doctors wanted to be aggressive in their treatment.

Dani's OB and oncologist recommended removing her uterus, and Dani insisted on harvesting her eggs first. Charlie had been in the hospital with Dani while she recovered when Betti visited. Betti had given birth to her fourth child a few years before. She had always boasted that she wanted a half dozen kids, but her husband was done after their fourth.

But he must not have had a problem with her being pregnant. Betti offered to serve as a surrogate for Dani's baby and said Mike was on board.

It all went quickly after that. Betti and Dani waited until the cancer was gone, and then Betti was carrying a child from Dani's eggs and a sperm donor. Betti was one of those people Charlie never understood who proclaimed to anyone and everyone that she loved being pregnant. From what Charlie saw, Betti definitely loved the attention that being a surrogate for her cousin who had cancer got her. Charlie couldn't understand loving the feeling of her body not being her own, morning sickness, or especially childbirth. She had briefly considered offering herself as a surrogate for Dani. Still, she was relieved when Betti made her proposal, and Dani accepted.

"Betti," Charlie said, "what are you up to today?" Charlie had learned over the years that some conversations were more manageable when she asked questions, turning the conversation back on the other person. She loved Betti and what she did to bring Rainna into the world, but that didn't mean Charlie enjoyed spending time with her. Family gatherings were enough.

"Oh, well." Betti shifted on her feet and tucked her hair behind her ears. "I'm not sure if Mama told you, but Mike

and I are trying out a temporary separation. It's no big deal."
She waved her hand like she was swatting a fly. "We'll have
everything worked out before you know it. We had a quick
meeting with the judge today about the kids."

"I hadn't heard. I'm sorry. I hope you two get it figured out.
You've been together pretty much as long as I can remember."

Betti and Mike had been together since they were thir-
teen, and the news that they were separated shocked Charlie.
She wanted to show Betti support, but she didn't want to be
caught up in an awkward conversation about marital issues.

A wide smile broke across Betti's face. "Hey, I've got the
best idea! My next appointment isn't for an hour. How about
you come back to the salon with me. I'll fix those hideous
nails of yours, and we can catch up! You can tell me all about
your newest recipes and if Rainna's thrown any food at you.
You can catch me up on what's new with my baby!"

If Betti and Mike were meeting with a judge about custody issues, it was more serious than Betti let on. Despite the
insult to her nails, Charlie could see Betti's excitement at the
prospect. Betti meant well, but she had no filter. Maybe the
time to chat and do Charlie's nails would give Betti a reprieve
from worrying about whatever was going on with her.

Charlie hadn't spent time alone with Betti since Dani's
death. Betti had babysat Rainna the night Dani died. After
Dani's death, Betti tried to get custody of Rainna. She said
that as the surrogate, and someone with experience caring
for Rainna, she had more of a right to her than anyone else.
And Betti was already a parent, so she wasn't starting from
scratch. Charlie had tried not to take it personally. Rainna
was great; anyone would want her. But it still stung when
she remembered Betti saying Charlie didn't know how to
care for Rainna.

Charlie was surprised that Betti read her blog—the crack about Rainna throwing food at her was from one of the stories Charlie shared on the blog. While her food blog was well-respected, she saw more uplift and interest after including honest and sometimes ridiculous stories along with recipes. Rainna only threw food at her once, and luckily it was only pea fritters and nothing with a sauce.

Charlie looked at her nails and saw the uneven edges and torn cuticles. She couldn't remember the last time she'd had her nails done. It was time.

"That sounds great, Betti. I'll meet you there in a couple minutes." Charlie didn't love the idea of an hour with Betti, but she was family.

"Really? Yay! You hardly ever let me fix you up. Okay, when you get there, head on back to my table. I'll grab my stuff from the back and meet you there. I fully expect you to spill on what you were doing this morning." Betti winked at Charlie and wiggled her eyebrows in a way that had Charlie chuckling despite herself. "Fingers crossed you were here to see that handsome Ethan and finally take him up on that date I heard he's been asking for." Rolling her eyes, Charlie jumped in the Jeep without looking at Betti.

Charlie drove the short distance down Main Street to the salon. She pushed open the heavy metal door to the back entrance that only Betti and the other stylists used.

The salon was divided by a series of paneled room dividers. The partitions looked like frosted glass with white silhouettes of tree branches giving the room a funky aesthetic. The salon was once an open space, but the owners bought the dividers because the stylists were sick of clients having conversations across the room. Now, the hair salon was on the right, and the nail salon was on the left. The back entrance came in on the nail side, which was empty, and chatter was coming from the hair side.

Charlie made her way to the wall of nail polish, immediately zeroing in on a cobalt blue called "You'll Never Be Royal." She made her way to the nail table cluttered with a bouquet of flowers, photos of her little cousins, and a photo of Betti, Dani, and Rainna that Charlie had snapped right after Rainna's birth.

She bent down to examine the photo and was struck with longing for her big sister. Dani looked happier than Charlie had ever seen her. She was holding Rainna and sitting on the hospital bed next to Betti. Her short dark hair was sticking up in weird places from waking up in the middle of the night and rushing to the hospital.

Charlie stayed with Dani the night Rainna arrived, and they were both there for the birth. On the way, Charlie gave Dani a shirt that said "Mama Bear" and a "Baby Bear" onesie for Rainna. They were wearing their matching outfits in the photo.

Charlie took a seat, fighting the tears that were threatening to spill and trying to swallow past the lump in her throat. She was still waiting on Betti when the voices from the hair side of the salon got louder. They were behind the partition, so she couldn't see them, but it sounded like older women.

"... not sure if you'd heard yet, but Earl told me this morning that Lanie Taylor got arrested last night."

"No!" two women said at the same time.

"Apparently, she rammed her car into Gene Garner's truck last night. He was at the stop sign by the Quickie Mart when she hit him." Charlie could hear in the woman's voice that she enjoyed sharing the information.

A woman who sounded like she'd been chain smoking her whole life piped in. "Now, is Lanie the one married to Ricky? Or is she Bobby's wife?"

"Vivienne, you know Lanie. She's Ricky's wife. She works in the principal's office over at the high school."

Charlie thought of a beautiful blonde woman playing with her kids at the park. After seeing Lanie there several times while Charlie was with Rainna, Charlie had introduced herself. They would often chitchat while the kids played.

She tried to keep her breathing as quiet as possible. If they had noticed her walk in, she knew they wouldn't be talking where she could listen.

"Girls, girls," the first speaker continued, in a no-nonsense tone that made Charlie recognize the speaker as her fourth-grade teacher, Mrs. Potter. Mrs. Potter had retired from teaching about a decade ago, but retirement hadn't slowed down her feisty streak. "Lanie didn't just get arrested for slamming her car into Gene's truck. She got arrested for what they found in her car."

Mrs. Potter paused dramatically, giving her friends time to chime in with, "Well…" and, "What did they find?"

"Earl told me when that cute police chief showed up he found a bottle of OxyContin and an open bottle of Chardonnay."

"No!" said Vivienne.

"Hmmm…" the third woman said. "That's interesting."

"Why did you say it like that?" Mrs. Potter asked. "What do you think you know that you're not telling us. Spill, Roberta."

When Mrs. Potter named the third speaker, Charlie realized that Roberta was the old school superintendent's widow. She hadn't recognized the voice because she hadn't seen her since she was in high school.

"Well," said Roberta, "my sister's son, Johnny was on that jury with Lanie."

"What jury?" Mrs. Potter asked.

"The one for that boy who killed the older Allen girl. I remember him griping about Ricky's wife. But then again, Johnny's always complaining about something. He said that if Ricky had done a better job of keeping that wife of his in line, that they would have come to a decision in under an hour. That she was the reason it took almost a whole day. Everyone was so mad that she was wasting their time."

Charlie's heart sped up. They were talking about Darius's trial.

"But she changed her mind in the end," Vivienne said.

Charlie was holding her breath, waiting for Roberta to continue.

"That she did. Johnny told me she argued hard against convicting that Black boy until after their dinner break. Everyone ate, took a bathroom break, and they took another vote. She voted to convict and never said another word."

Mrs. Potter and Vivienne started talking at the same time. "You don't think…" "Could she have…" They laughed, and Mrs. Potter continued, "Could she have been taking drugs in the jury room? Maybe took something that made her stop caring."

"I could ask Johnny to be sure, but my money's on…"

"Charlie!"

Charlie jerked at the sound of Betti's loud voice, knocking a bottle of nail polish and a picture of Betti's oldest to the floor. Luckily, the glass on the bottle was thick enough that it didn't break, and the picture frame was plastic.

Charlie pasted a smile on her face as she turned to her cousin, trying to calm her racing heart. "Did you get lost?

I beat you here by twenty minutes." Charlie was impressed with how calm her voice sounded when she spoke.

"Oh, hush," Betti said with a wave of her hand. "You know it was only ten. I was outta gas. Now, let's get those awful cuticles soaking, and you can tell me everything new with you."

Charlie took a shaky breath, listening for more of the conversation she'd been eavesdropping on. She only heard a hairdryer.

Could Lanie have been medicated during the trial?

Charlie tried to keep her mind on Betti when she dipped her fingers in the warm bowl.

"Nothing's new with me," she lied. In the last twenty-four hours, Charlie's life had been twisted up more than she was the one time she'd gone to yoga class. "Tell me what's going on with you."

CHAPTER 5

Betti's chatter flowed around Charlie like the wind at the beach, never relenting. She tried to enjoy the feel of the warm water on her cuticles and the rhythm of the nail file. Betti had used the time to fill Charlie in on all the extracurriculars her boys were in, and she gave Charlie a new list of parenting recommendations for Rainna.

Something about a salon encouraged women to spill secrets. Charlie hated small-town gossip, having seen too many good people hurt by rumors, including her. But today, she couldn't get her mind off the story of Lanie and she was itching to know more.

"Hey, Betti, do you know Ricky's wife, Lanie?" Ricky Taylor was a little older than Charlie but younger than Betti. In high school, he had been an all-state running back, so most people in the area knew him. Now he owned a few rental properties out by the lake. If Charlie remembered correctly, he and Lanie met his first year of college when he was on a football scholarship and she was on the volleyball team. They had two kids a little older than Rainna.

"I take it you heard about her crash then," Betti replied conspiratorially. "That's all anyone wants to talk about this morning. I ran into her with her lawyer when I was down at the courthouse earlier. Lookin' a little worse for wear after a night in jail. The judge set bail, and she was headed home. A total mess."

"If they kept her overnight, it must have been more than just a wreck," Charlie said.

"Drugs," Betti replied. "Stoned out of her mind when it happened. It's probably why she wasn't hurt—bein' so relaxed and all."

"I don't know Lanie well. But she's always kind and seems like she has it together," Charlie said. They had talked a few times while their kids played at the park. Lanie didn't seem like someone who would take drugs. And had Lanie really been against convicting Darius? Or was it an exaggeration for a good story after a bad accident?

"Oh, girl! You're so naive. About a quarter of the ladies coming in here are taking something for their 'anxiety.'" She shook her head and continued, her voice in a loud whisper. "Honestly, Darius probably got them started in the first place."

"Wait, Darius? What do you mean?"

"Didn't you ever hear?" she asked with a smirk as she finished putting the top coat on Charlie's nails. "It was all over town when he was first arrested. He was a drug rep for one of those pharmaceutical companies. I heard that he was selling his stuff on the side."

"What?" Charlie asked. "That can't be true. Wouldn't that be easy to track?"

Betti pursed her lips to the side and raised her shoulders in a shrug. "I don't know anything about that. I'm just repeating what I've heard." She moved Charlie to position her hands in the infrared dryer while chatting about a girl from Charlie's year in school and how cute her new baby was.

A few minutes later, Betti reached over and tapped Charlie's nails. "Alrighty girl, you're all done! Those nails look fabulous. I expect you to take good care of them."

Charlie could see Betti's half smile as she looked at Charlie's nails. It had been a strange morning, but Charlie was grateful for Betti's warmth and the face time with another adult. It was easy for her to fall into a rhythm of work and Rainna without seeing others around town.

A bell chimed and Betti waved to the front of the shop where her next appointment had just walked in.

Charlie took the arrival of someone new as her cue to head out. "Thanks so much, Betti. These look great. I really appreciate it, and Rain's gonna be super jealous."

"Anytime, girl. Bring my baby by soon and I'll fix her nails, too!" she said as Charlie headed out the door.

Charlie was able to get in a run with Buck and finish her posts for her website and social media before it was time to pick up Rainna. On the drive home from school, they sang at the top of their lungs with both of them missing more words than they got right.

"Sweets, I'm not working on any recipes tonight, so you get to pick dinner," Charlie told Rainna as they were getting out of the Jeep and heading up the front steps.

"Pizza!" Rainna squealed and Charlie laughed.

"Okay, pizza it is. Let me guess. You want salad on it?" Charlie teased.

"No salad!" Rainna insisted. "I want cheese, and pepperoni, and sausage, and meatballs!"

"I guess I'll let you have all of your favorite toppings, but you have to let me put veggies on it."

"Ugh," Rainna said with a huff.

Charlie knew that Rainna was only pretending to be mad because Charlie always chopped the veggies so small that Rainna could barely tell they were there.

"But I get to help," Rainna said with a smile.

Once Charlie got the pizza in the oven, she turned around and surveyed the kitchen. Buck was trying to gobble up the dropped food before he was shooed out of the kitchen. "Rainna, there is cheese all over my floor, you silly girl!" Rainna giggled and ran. Charlie pretended to chase her and then knelt to clean the food off the floor.

Buck ran to the door and started barking right as Charlie heard three quick knocks.

She pulled the door open to see Ethan Williams leaning against the railing of her front porch. He was still wearing his uniform, and he didn't have a blond hair out of place. He was tall and fit and his blue eyes were on Charlie.

"Charlie," he said in a low voice and she felt a flush of heat on her neck. Seeing him made her feel like she was sixteen and it always took her a moment to remember that those days were almost half a lifetime ago.

"Ethan. What are you doing here?" she asked. In the last few years that she had been back in town, he had made it a somewhat regular occurrence to drop by her house unannounced. He was her first love and her first heartbreak. And while she liked him as a person, she wasn't interested in more, so she tried to keep her interactions with him as blunt as possible.

"No, 'it's great to see you, thanks for stopping by, why don't you come on in'? Come on, Charlie. You were raised better than that. You don't want to be a bad role model for Rainna, do you?" he said, and his arrow hit the target. Everything she had done for the last three years was about Rainna.

"Sorry, Ethan. It's great to see you. Thanks for stopping by." She repeated his words but in a much warmer tone than when she answered the door.

"Auntie!" Rainna yelled from the kitchen. "Dinner's ready!" She darted into the kitchen to get the pizza before it burned, pulling the pizza off the stone with her peel.

"Smells delicious," Ethan said from the other side of the kitchen. He was wearing a smile like a wildcatter who'd just discovered oil. "You know your pizza is my favorite." He shifted his smile to Rainna. "Rainna, what do you think? Is there enough here for me, too?"

"Yes!" Rainna said. "Auntie always makes lots." She had an excited smile as she looked up at her aunt.

"Alright," Charlie replied while feeling a prickle of annoyance. Ethan loved to show up right when she was making dinner and then weasel a way to stay. Charlie knew he loved her cooking, but there was more to it. Still, she never complained. The main reason Charlie stayed in town was so Rainna could be around people who knew and loved her.

The house got quiet as they all tucked into their dinner. Charlie tried to get Ethan to say what brought him by, but he said, "Little ears," while Rainna wasn't looking.

Ethan and Rainna played cops and robbers while Charlie cleaned up after dinner. Rainna made him be the robber because she thought it was funny for a cop to be a bad guy. Then, Charlie put Rainna to bed a little early so she could talk to Ethan.

"Anything to drink?" she asked him as she came back downstairs. He was sitting on the couch watching a football game.

"I'm good," he replied with a glance over his shoulder. "Why don't you come sit by me?"

Charlie took a seat in the chair instead of the open spot by Ethan on the couch. "To what do I owe the pleasure, Ethan?" she asked.

Ethan lowered the volume on the television and turned to face her. "I talked to Winnie today."

"And?" Charlie asked. She had guessed her conversation with Winnie prompted this visit. Without knowing what Winnie said, she didn't want to give away more than she needed to.

"Well, she said y'all had a talk, and you mentioned to her that you couldn't remember much about the trial. She said you might have a few questions for me. In case you were too embarrassed to ask me yourself, I thought I'd make it easier for you."

"Why would I be embarrassed?" she asked, hating that Ethan felt he could put labels on her emotions.

"Not embarrassed," he started to backpedal but then he stopped. "But Charlie, you don't like to let anyone think you're not perfect. You do everything by yourself, and you never ask for help. If you have questions, ask them."

"Fine." He was right that she didn't like to ask for help. She never had. After she had gotten divorced and dropped out of law school, her dad seemed so disappointed in her that she never wanted him or anyone else to see if things didn't work out perfectly. She couldn't handle, "I told you so."

She also wasn't ready for this conversation. Charlie was a planner. Driving to the courthouse today had been impulsive and out of character. When she did something, she wanted to be ready. But Ethan was here, so she had to make the most of it.

"Did Darius confess?" she asked her biggest question first, hoping she might catch him off guard.

"Where did you hear that?" he asked, sounding every bit the chief trying to stop a leak in his department.

"Doesn't matter. Did he?" she asked as she leaned toward him.

"You know I can't answer that." He leaned back on the couch, crossed his arms, and squinted at her.

"Okay, okay. What would you ask if our roles were reversed?" she said, trying to keep the mood light, despite the topic.

"Char, if our roles were reversed, I would trust that you did your job and move on." He ran a hand across his face. "But I know we look at things differently, so I would ask what evidence there was."

She nodded. Ethan would trust that she had done her job if he was in her position. "So, tell me about the evidence."

"He was caught speeding only a few miles away right around the time it happened. His DNA was all over her. And he was seen leaving her house not long before someone spotted the smoke." She stayed silent, hoping he would give her more, but he didn't continue.

Ethan uncrossed his arms and the expression on his face softened. "He did it, Char. I'm not sure what happened between them that night, but he did it. He must have gone into a rage. He raped her and then hit her over the head hard enough to kill her. Then, he got freaked out and used what was around the house to light the place on fire. He sped out of there, not thinking anyone would see him. But someone did. And then, Harvey caught him speeding. The investigation went fast because it was a sloppy crime. We looked at other people, but it was Darius." He reached over to place his hand on her shoulder.

Charlie tried to ignore his touch as she remembered Darius's accusation that it could have been Dani's ex-boyfriend who worked in the same hospital. Charlie took a deep breath, "What about Liam?" He removed his hand from her shoulder as his eyebrows drew together.

The one time Charlie was supposed to meet Dani's ex, Dr. Liam Sullivan, he had canceled on them at the last minute with no excuse, cementing his status as a tool in Charlie's mind. The last time Dani broke up with him, she mentioned a scene at the hospital where he had grabbed her arm in front of some of their coworkers. Charlie suspected that if he was bold enough to grab her in public, he was probably worse in private.

"It wasn't him."

"Okay," Charlie dragged out the word in her annoyance that he didn't give her more, but she didn't want to fight. "I heard about a patient at the hospital who hassled Dani because he thought he was Rainna's sperm donor. Did you ever look into him?" she asked.

He relaxed back onto the couch. "If that happened, no one has ever talked to me about it in the last three years. But I can tell you that I did ask her coworkers about any patients. There was no one significant."

She racked her brain for something else. "Wait," she held up a finger, "one more. Is there any truth to the rumor that Lanie was taking drugs in the jury room?"

His jaw clenched and he sat forward, "I thought you knew better than to believe rumors." The question made his demeanor change. He no longer looked like her friend but like the army soldier he had been after high school. "Let me be clear; I hate rumors. I thought you did, too. Lanie has nothing to do with you or your sister's case."

Holding his gaze, she saw him soften. "Why are you bothering yourself with this? I know how to do my job. It's been three years. A jury convicted him. You're not a cop. You're not even a lawyer. What good is all this? You need to stop." He rubbed at his temples and shook his head as he rose.

Charlie bit the inside of her cheek to keep herself quiet. She had left law school because she wanted to not because she couldn't cut it. But for some reason people always saw that as a failure.

"Thanks for dinner. I'm heading out. I know this time of year's hard for you. My offer to talk is still on the table, as long as you don't plan on dragging up baseless rumors. Goodnight." He leaned down to kiss her cheek and walked to the door.

The door slammed behind him, and Charlie moved from the chair to sprawl across the couch, looking at the wall and the marks on it where her grandparents had kept track of the heights of all their kids and grandkids. Charlie thought about what Ethan had said about Darius and all roads pointing to him. But she couldn't stop coming back to the fact that he didn't know anything about the patient and he wouldn't tell her why he thought Dani's ex didn't do it. Not to mention the fact that he didn't say that Lanie hadn't been taking drugs.

CHAPTER 6

———

Charlie was out of breath as she wiped the sweat from her brow after her morning run. Buck was panting as he ran to lap water out of his bowl. Charlie guzzled her water and pulled out her phone. After a quick internet search, she dialed a number and pressed send.

Her run had been clouded with thoughts of her conversations with Winnie, Betti, Ethan, and the women she overheard at the salon. Ethan was sure of the investigation, and she had no reason to believe Darius over him. But exercise had brought her some clarity, and she decided to share some information in an effort to do the right thing.

What Betti told Charlie about Darius dealing drugs bothered her, but it was far-fetched, and she didn't see how it could be true. That was the kind of thing that people latched on to and used as proof of bad character.

The rumor about Lanie in the jury room, however, felt like it held a kernel of truth. Ethan shutting her questioning down about Lanie and reminding her it wasn't her job to look into this made her think there was more to the story.

Charlie's fingers were itching to dial Winnie to talk about Ethan and Lanie. But she knew what Winnie would say. Winnie would tell her that whether or not Lanie took drugs while on the jury wasn't her problem. And Winnie would be right. But that didn't mean Charlie could let it go.

She knew Darius's lawyer was responsible for looking into things like this, but if they didn't know, how could they do anything about it? And if Charlie kept this information to herself, what did that mean about her? She may not have finished law school, but she respected the justice system and believed in fair trials. Charlie didn't know who Darius's lawyer was or how to get in touch with them, but she knew how to get in touch with his brother.

"Thomas Realty, how may I direct your call?" a pleasant female voice asked.

"Malachi Thomas," Charlie said, still out of breath from her run.

"Miss, I believe Mr. Thomas is in a meeting. Can I take a message and have him get back to you?"

"Could you please let him know that Charlie Allen is on the phone?"

"Miss, I'll let him know you called. Does he have your number?" Charlie got the impression from the woman's tone that she didn't like it when others didn't immediately comply with her requests.

Charlie tried to keep her voice as pleasant as possible. "Could you please let him know that Charlie Allen is on the phone?" she repeated.

"Well, if you insist. It would be a lot simpler if you just let me give him a message to call you back," the receptionist said. "I'm going to put you on hold now."

The line was filled with an instrumental version of one of Charlie's favorite songs from the nineties. Despite the call she was making, she found herself dancing and humming along to the Hanson's "MMMBop."

"Charlie?" a deep voice asked as the music cut off. Charlie had seen Darius's brother, Malachi, at the trial, but she had never spoken to him. She imagined the tall dark man with a short beard, who wore impeccable suits and walked with an air of authority.

Silence filled the line, and Charlie's mind went blank. She knew she should say something, but she was having difficulty finding the right words.

A heavy sigh came through the line. "It's the letters. Isn't it?" he said. When she didn't answer, he continued. "I didn't know about it until after he sent the first one. I tried to tell him he shouldn't send anything to you. I was furious when I found out he sent another one." He spoke quickly. "I can't believe he sent you a third. He wants you to believe him, and he doesn't know how else to reach you."

Malachi tried to talk Darius out of sending the letters? Charlie stood holding the phone. She felt ridiculous. She had made this call, and now she couldn't find words to string together.

"Wait," he started, sounding unsure of himself, "My assistant just said Charlie Allen. That's probably a common name. This is Charlie, Charlotte Allen, right?"

"Yes," she said, clearing her throat. Something about him sounding confused and unsure pulled her back to herself. "I'm sorry, I didn't mean to make you think you had someone else. Well, actually, it's not really the letters." She paused, not sure how to tell him the real reason for her call.

She thought he would be the type of man who always filled the empty spaces in conversations, but he waited for her to continue. "I did read the letters—when the third one came. I hadn't been able to before. I don't know what I think about what he said. I don't know him. But I do know some of the people who looked into Dani's murder, and I have no reason not to believe them." She stopped herself from rambling. "That's not why I called."

"Okay," Malachi said calmly, "why did you call?"

"Two reasons," she started. "One is a question I wanted to ask you. The other is a rumor that I thought you should know. You can pick which one to start with. But if you need to go, I understand." As Darius's brother, he would be able to pass along any information she gave him to Darius's lawyer. Malachi owned a successful real estate business in the Dallas area. She had heard of his company when she moved to Dallas after leaving Austin and law school. If he had really been in a meeting, like his assistant said, she should allow him to get off the phone. If he did, she wouldn't call back.

"From what I hear, I have you to thank for making sure that Darius didn't get the death penalty. If that's true, I can't imagine there would be a time that I wouldn't be willing to talk to you."

"Question or rumor?" she asked him again, avoiding the question implied in Malachi's reply. She didn't want to talk about that. Her insistence that the DA not pursue the death penalty had nothing to do with Darius. One of her law professors had constantly talked about the death penalty: how much it cost the system, how unfairly it was applied, how there were issues with procuring the drugs to administer it. All those things had stuck with her. She had been opposed to it for several years, never thinking it would touch her life.

When it did, she wasn't going to back down on her beliefs, even when it was hard.

"Rumor," Malachi said, "who knows, hearing this might affect my answer to your question."

Charlie took a deep breath and pulled her sweat-soaked shirt away from her body. She was warm before the run, but now the shirt felt cold, and she wished she had taken the time to change.

"One of the jurors in the trial was recently arrested after a car accident," she tried to keep her tone steady. "It may have been caused by prescription drug use, and it may have been going on for a while."

Her heart was racing. She was trying not to overthink the implications of what she had just done. While Darius's attorney would need more information and actual evidence, she had given information that could potentially open the door for Darius to make an appeal. She had also done something the people in her town would most definitely not approve of. But what bothered her the most was that she was sharing a rumor about someone she liked, even if she didn't know her well.

There was a long pause before he spoke. "When you say a while... are you saying one of the jurors was taking drugs during the trial?" There was a touch of anger in his voice, but it sounded like he was working hard to stay composed.

"Maybe," she ran a hand over her face. "Look, I'm struggling with this. I don't know if Darius did it. But if so, I just gave you a piece of information that might get him a new trial. That's terrifying." Her hands shaking, she continued, "I never want to go through that again. Or to put Rainna through that. But I believe in doing the right thing, even when it's hard. I just hope this is the right thing."

She expected questions from him, but instead, he said, "What was your question?"

Charlie swallowed, "Did he confess?"

"What?" She fumbled her phone as his voice boomed. "What are you talking about? Darius did not confess. He's said he's innocent from day one. Why would someone take the stand at their own trial if they had already confessed?"

"Well then, I guess you should know that my question was also a rumor," she worked her bottom lip between her teeth, not knowing what else to say.

"Wow." The line went silent and Charlie waited for him to continue. "Where did this come from?" he asked.

"I hadn't heard about it until recently. From what I can tell, it's known around town, but people never talked to me about it." She ran her hand over her head. She had become an outsider in her hometown, and she wasn't sure what to do with that. Was she just in the dark about Dani's death? Was this because she'd kept to herself since moving back? Or something else?

"I'm sorry," Malachi told her in a comforting voice. It felt like he was sitting across from her instead of a couple hundred miles away.

"Why?" she asked. Was he sorry for Darius? This conversation was not going the way she thought it would. She had expected questions and maybe anger toward her.

"I'm sorry you feel like you've been left in the dark on something so important to you. I'm sorry you have to make decisions about sharing information with people you don't know or have any reason to trust."

Charlie had never been great with emotions, especially not her own. How was it that this man she was speaking to for the first time could understand her so well? She wanted to have someone to talk this through with, but if Winnie and Ethan and even Betti had been keeping details about all of this from her, who could she turn to? Before she leaned into the feeling of being understood and spilled her guts to a total stranger, she decided to cut off the call. "Well, I better be going, and I'm sure you've got a busy day. I pulled you away from a meeting. I'm sorry."

"Charlie." Malachi's voice was full of authority and she could understand how he could build a realty company from the ground up with dozens of employees. "Before you hang up, get a pen." He paused for a few seconds before giving her his cell phone number. "You may never need or want it, but now you have it in case you do."

"Oh, Malachi," Charlie said, remembering Darius's letters. "Darius said there was something in the transcript that caught his attention. Do you know what it was?"

"Hmm... I'm not sure if this is it, but I know for a while he was hung up on the arson experts. But I could ask."

"Okay, thanks. I appreciate it."

"Charlie, I know you didn't ask my opinion, but I don't think Darius did it. I think if you'd met him before all this, you never would have believed it either. They hadn't been together long, but he was crazy about Dani. The way he talked to me about her—well, I thought she was it for him."

Charlie thought back to what she knew about Darius before all this happened. Dani had met him when he was visiting some doctors at the hospital she worked at for his job as a pharmaceutical sales rep. Dani said he immediately asked her out for that night. She said she didn't have time for a date and he said if she would agree, he would figure something out. He ran to the vending machine, bought one of everything and laid a spread out before her. The moment her shift was over, they had their first date in the hospital waiting room. They had been dating about two months and he made the three-hour drive to see her once or twice a week.

"Thank you, Malachi," Charlie said clearing her throat.

"Bye, Charlie."

"Bye."

Charlie hung up the phone and eased down to sit on the kitchen floor, wondering how badly she was going to regret that call tomorrow.

CHAPTER 7

Dew was still on the grass and the air had the crispness of fall on Monday morning when Charlie went to the courthouse to fill out a request for a copy of the transcript. She'd gone first thing in the morning, trying to avoid too many nosy people. But the clerk, herself, was very interested in the request and Charlie knew it wouldn't stay a secret.

It took a week for the clerk to get her copy ready, and she had to pay by the page.

In the two weeks since she'd gotten it, she had read all the way through twice and was thoroughly disappointed. If she was honest, she hadn't expected anything crazy to jump out and tell her one way or the other if Darius did it, but it was still annoying.

The first time she read through it was tough. She tried to pay attention but found herself getting lost in words, imagining Dani's fear or pain. By the end of the transcript, she didn't know much more than when she started.

The next time she read through it, she tried to take herself out of the equation. If she thought about her personal tie to the case, she would never get anywhere. It was just another true crime case. She had to think of it as one of the cases on a podcast or documentary.

Telling herself that it wasn't personal worked, somewhat. She was able to read through the testimony and retain it. But it was still hard to grasp. Nothing stood out as proof that Darius did or didn't do it.

Neither side presented many witnesses. The trial only took two weeks. The prosecution focused on Darius as a person and involved a lot of conjecture and speculation. The defense objected constantly but was almost always overruled.

The defense put their trust in expert witnesses, whose testimony was technical and dry. Understanding the jargon was harder than box jumping at CrossFit with her ex. Each expert's testimony made it seem like anyone would be stupid not to see things exactly the way they did.

When she finished reading through the transcript the second time, she threw the papers across the room in frustration. How many times could she read about her sister's death? It was wrong, but she felt this tug inside to keep looking, to keep trying to understand what happened.

She had spent her free time looking into this recently and didn't feel any closer to answers. Reading the transcript was the strange way she passed her time now, before Rainna woke up in the mornings, in any extra time during her day, and before bed.

Her gut told her something was there, in the pages, just beyond her comprehension. Because even as she had read Darius's letters, she wondered if they were true. While she wasn't seeing anything in the pages that cleared Darius, she also wasn't seeing anything that made him seem all that guilty. If he did it, shouldn't it be more obvious? Malachi said Darius mentioned something to do with the arson expert testimony, so she looked at that. But it was very technical. And she couldn't understand why two experts, looking at the same scene had such different opinions.

The sound of pawing pulled her attention away from the pages. "Buck! Get off my Anna dress!" Charlie told him when she noticed he had curled up on her Halloween costume. She had set her dress and Rainna's Elsa costume on the table, but they had fallen and Buck had made himself a bed. Charlie would prefer not to be picking black dog hairs off her costume all night while at the elementary school's Halloween fundraiser carnival. But the hairs would probably get there anyway with Buck accompanying them. Rainna wasn't in elementary school yet, but the carnival was a town tradition.

Rainna spent the last week talking about how her friend's family was dressing as the cast of *The Incredibles* for Halloween. Charlie felt so much guilt over Rainna not having a big family that she promised to do a family costume with Rainna. Luckily the carnival was taking place outside because Rainna wanted to dress Buck up as a reindeer. Rainna also planned to carry a stuffed snowman to make the costume complete. Charlie had to take a stuffed Christof doll.

Once she got the dresses off the floor, Charlie glanced at the clock. *Crap.* They needed to leave in twenty minutes and they hadn't even started getting ready. She shuffled the papers into a folder and tucked them away.

"Rainna! We're about to be late. Let's get your dress on."

"Auntie." Rainna bunny-hopped down the stairs. "Stop yelling! We get to be princesses tonight!" she continued in a sing-song voice as Charlie lunged to tickle her. Rainna's perpetual cheer was enough to distract Charlie from her frustration.

After thirty minutes of getting dressed, braiding hair, and wrestling Buck into reindeer horns, they were ready to go get some candy.

They parked the Jeep and got out. High-pitched shrieks and laughter filled the air along with the smells of hot dogs, cooking oil, and burnt popcorn. The air was crisp from a cold front earlier in the week, but with their long sleeves and tights, they were okay.

The Halloween carnival took place in a blocked-off parking lot at the elementary school. It was filled with booths from school clubs trying to raise money for uniforms, travel, equipment, and more. Parents and cars were dressed in themes for trunk or treat for the smaller kids. The carnival also included booths for locals who were up for election.

Rainna found Winnie's youngest, Sarah, almost immediately. They went off in a group to collect their candy and play club games for the chance to win cheap prizes bought in bulk. Buck kept tugging on his lead, trying to get to the dropped candy and food littering the ground.

"Why is it you always get to be a princess, and I'm stuck being a witch?" Winnie asked as Charlie made her way over and Winnie looked down at her own flowing black robe.

"You're always a princess and you know it. Also, trust me, I'm going to have to deal with little girls coming up to me all night telling me which sister is their favorite. You got off better in the costume game."

"Hey." Winnie grabbed Charlie's forearm. "Tom asked me to tell you that he should have everything with your dad's estate wrapped up in the next few weeks. Selling the house covered the last of the medical bills and there was a little bit left over. I still can't believe he was paying bills from your mom's illness all this time," Winnie said shaking her head.

Charlie shrugged. "I didn't know either. He kept me in the dark."

"Hey." Winnie stopped walking and looked at Charlie. "I know I shouldn't speak ill of the dead," she looked over to where the girls were playing and lowered her voice, "but your dad was a dick with the way he treated you all these years. You didn't do anything wrong."

Charlie laughed; Winnie had been a mom for so long now that she always whispered when she called someone a name if kids were around.

"I still can't believe he missed your graduation, all because he was pissed about that stupid rumor about you and Ethan after prom. And that he tried to take Rainna just because he didn't want you to have her. He was a horrible dad after your mom died."

"I know. I know." Charlie waved her hand. "But that doesn't mean that dealing with his death has been easy. Rainna still misses going to his place every other weekend for the court-ordered visitation. Now that she doesn't have a male figure in her life, I feel like she's latching on to Ethan."

Winnie raised her eyebrows. "That doesn't sound like a bad thing to me."

They made their way through booths and games, waving to people they knew along the way. "Oh, hey, you didn't tell me you got a copy of the transcript," Winnie said to Charlie as they followed the kids.

Charlie wasn't surprised that Winnie knew. Nothing stayed hidden in a small town.

Charlie shrugged, wanting it to seem like it wasn't a big deal. "I was sick of not remembering the trial and feeling like everybody else knows things that I didn't."

"Have you been through it yet?" Winnie reached up and rubbed Charlie's shoulder.

"Yeah." Charlie tugged on the end of her side braid. "It was tough. I wish I could keep Dani in my mind the way she was the last time I visited. Reading through all that changes it."

Winnie's arm came back up and wrapped around Charlie's middle as she leaned her head into her shoulder. The showing of affection was rare because she usually gave Charlie the personal space Charlie preferred.

"Sarah! Get back here right now!" The moment of comfort was broken by Winnie's daughter weaving her way through the crowd to get closer to the animals in the petting zoo set up by the FFA, the organization formerly known as the Future Farmers of America. Sarah didn't listen and was petting a baby goat when they finally made it through the crowd to where she stood. Winnie went with the girls to pet the animals while Charlie hung back with Buck and watched.

When they finished at the petting zoo and Sarah promised not to make a break for it again, Winnie circled back to their conversation. "Did you find what you were looking for in the transcript?"

"No," Charlie answered honestly.

"Ethan told me y'all talked. But he wouldn't say how it went, so I'm guessing not well."

"It was fine."

Winnie tilted her head like she wanted to say something. After a few moments, she said, "You know, it wouldn't be the worst thing to let people know what's going on in that head of yours. To let people in a little bit."

Charlie watched the toes of her black converse peek out from beneath the green skirt of her dress to avoid looking at Winnie. She was right. Charlie pushed people away. She hadn't let anyone new get close to her since she and her ex divorced, and she wasn't even good at it back then.

"Auntie!" Rainna slammed into Charlie's legs before she saw her coming. "The basketball team set up a maze for kids with hay bales. Can Sarah and I go? Please, please, please?"

"Can I come with you?" Charlie asked.

"No, Auntie! You're too big. It's just for kids." She had her tiny fists on her hips and was giving Charlie her best puppy dog eyes.

"Win, is it okay with you?"

"Of course. Get going, girls."

"Rain, stay with Sarah. Wait for me at the end. I'll meet you there."

Rainna let Charlie kiss the top of her head before she raced to the maze.

"I need to check on West. Can you get the girls and meet me back at the fishing booth?" Winnie's son West was helping at one of the booths they hadn't gotten to yet.

"Sure. See you in a few."

Charlie tugged Buck's lead to start the short walk over to the end of the maze when she heard a familiar voice.

"I do believe I see Miss Charlotte Allen. If you'll excuse me, Mrs. Schaefer." *Oh no.* Charlie watched George Marshall, the county DA, make his way toward her, so she plastered a fake smile on her face.

"Miss Charlotte. You sure are looking lovely tonight. Where is that beautiful charge of yours?" From her height, a few inches higher than his own, it looked like his hair was thinning even more than the last time she had seen him. Everyone else at the carnival was either dressed in costumes or casually. But George was wearing a blue suit and red tie, looking exactly like the politician he was.

"She's in the maze with some friends. I'm just walking around to meet her at the exit."

"I'll walk with you. I haven't seen you since your father's funeral. How long's it been?" He reached like he wanted to pat her shoulder in comfort but Charlie saw it coming and reached down to adjust Buck's costume, avoiding George's touch.

"Almost a year." Charlie pushed a loose strand of hair out of her face.

"Sad business, that. A good man but never quite the same after your lovely mother died." George looked over at Charlie like she was little orphan Annie rather than a grown woman. Charlie thought about her mother, the image of a kind and beautiful woman fading as Charlie had now lived longer without her than with her.

Charlie's father, however, was still clear in her mind, along with his disapproval of anything that didn't line up with his strict standards. Outside of condolences at her father's funeral, the last time she had spoken with George was when she approached him about not asking for the death penalty. He insisted her father join them. Their conversation got heated when he said that a sweet young girl like her, who couldn't even finish law school, had no business making decisions about something like that. Her father was firmly on George's side. Outside of pleasantries when her dad visited Rainna, she never had another conversation with him before he died.

When she didn't respond, George continued. "I was sorry to see the rift that the trial caused between you and your daddy." She turned her head so he wouldn't see her rolling her eyes. He had probably never taken the time to notice, but Charlie and her father's rift had not started, nor did it end, after the trial.

"Now, I know you think that you did what was right, asking that he only get life, but I still agree with your daddy on that one," he said. "But as you know, being an old friend of his, I couldn't let y'all's family drama become public. It was more important to me to protect your family, and letting you win that one was the best way. But I sure do wish that man was on death row right now."

CHAPTER 8

———

Charlie closed her eyes and took a deep breath to tamp down her annoyance. It was hard for Charlie to hear that an elected official would so flippantly say he wished a man was on death row, even if he was a murderer.

She let out her breath in a sigh as they reached the end of the maze and Rainna and Sarah came running out. They were giggling and giving each other high-fives. Charlie smiled and waved, readying herself to get away from George.

"Can we go again?" the girls yelled at the same time. Charlie groaned inwardly but nodded and kept her eyes on them until they made it back to the entrance.

George was still standing beside Charlie and she moved her gaze back to him. She thought he was waiting for her to say something, but she had nothing to say as she raised her eyes to his.

"Miss Charlotte, I realize I completely forgot my manners. I dove right in talking about your daddy, and I didn't even ask how you've been or how your little job is going. I still can't believe anyone with grades like yours would drop out of law school to write about food and post pictures on the internet for strangers." He paused and shook his head. "But what do I know? I'd starve without someone to cook for me."

"I'm enjoying the job. I've got a cookbook coming out next winter. It's still fun and challenging and I love the creativity of it. I never felt those things with the law, but I hope everything is going okay for you at the prosecutor's office." Charlie didn't care about his office, but she had forgotten her manners as well, and Nana would have threatened to take a switch after her for not being polite in conversation. She also wanted to be clear with him that what she did had value. Her chosen vocation wasn't a step down, just a step in a different direction.

"Glad to hear it. A cookbook! Good for you!"

Charlie clenched her jaw. She was successful at what she did, but his patronization stung.

"It's been pretty boring down at the office. Nothing too exciting happening lately. No good cases. But my wife made your coffee cake for me again last weekend," he said, rubbing his generous middle. "Delicious, as always. I do believe she said something about making one of your new recipes, a caramel apple s'mores dip, for the grandkids this weekend. My wife and I worry about you and that sweet girl all by yourselves in that big house."

Charlie looked at him and tilted her head. "I'm glad you like the cake, and I hope the grandkids like the dip. You'll have to tell Mrs. Marshall thank you for me. I'm grateful that she reads the blog. And I appreciate your concern, but Rainna and I are more than capable of taking care of ourselves." She wasn't sure if he had a reason for his concern, or if it was just something men of a certain generation liked to say.

"Now, I always enjoy seeing you, but let me get to the real reason I caught up to you. I want to make sure that that boy's lawyer hasn't been bothering you. Because I sure wouldn't want that," George said.

"That boy? Do you mean Darius Thomas?" At his nod, she shook her head, "No. Why?"

"I heard that lawyer of his has been digging around again." She felt him watching her closely and did her best to keep her features neutral.

"Couple of people on the jury said she's called asking questions." He leaned close to Charlie and lowered his voice. Charlie noticed that he smelled like butterscotch candy. "A waste of time if you ask me. That man's going to die in prison. But I guess that rich brother of his can spend his money how he wants."

Charlie thought of the letter she had received a week ago, sitting next to the other letters in her drawer. This new one was shorter than the others. But she knew the man beside her would be furious if he knew about the message from Darius thanking her for reading his letters. She had opened it immediately this time rather than waiting years. She was also sure that George wouldn't like the text message on her phone from Darius's brother.

She knew she should respond to George's statement. That's what a victim's family member would do when they received information like this. She felt the bite of the wind through the thin fabric of her costume and pulled her cloak tighter. "What's the lawyer talking to the jurors about?"

"Oh, just making stuff up. Trying to claim unfair deliberations. Like I said, nothing for you to worry about. I've got it all covered. That man's never going to see the outside of prison." This time he reached up to rub her shoulder before she had a chance to step away. She stood there awkwardly fighting revulsion and waiting for him to move his hand, afraid if she tried to shrug it off, he might move his hand up to her neck.

Growing up, she had always known George as one of her dad's friends. When she mentioned to her dad that she was thinking about law school during one of their brief truces, he insisted she ask George to write one of her letters of recommendation. George gladly wrote the letter. He even asked her to come back after her first year for an internship.

It didn't take long for Charlie working in the prosecutor's office to hear rumors. The legal secretary and receptionist warned Charlie to keep doors open and people nearby when George was around. For a part of the state that had more male attorneys, George's office tended to have more females, and usually pretty ones. She had seen his attempts at flirtations with those in the office more than once. She also heard from other staff that there were several affairs. While he had never tried anything overt with her, she was always hyperaware when he tried to touch her, which seemed like it happened more frequently than it should.

A bark at her side alerted her that the girls were headed her way.

"It looks like the girls are done with the maze, so I better meet back up with Winnie over by her son's booth. Thank you for updating me on the case, Mr. Marshall."

"Call me George. Mr. Marshall was my father. And you keep making delicious recipes, and my stomach will keep thanking you for them. You take care of that little one."

George stepped forward like he was going to hug her, but Buck pulled on Charlie's arm to get closer to Rainna. Charlie backed away with a wave. Buck licked Rainna's face as Sarah scratched his ears.

They met up with Winnie and made their way to the trunk or treat area. In between taking pictures of the girls, Charlie analyzed her conversation with George. He had no reason to think she was in contact with Malachi or Darius, and it was a secret she wasn't ready to share. It was a normal part of his job to keep the victim's family informed. Still, a small part of her worried. The clerk at the courthouse was sure to share that Charlie had requested a copy of the transcript.

Rainna's teeth were chattering as they finished getting candy from all the decorated vehicles. "Hey, Win. We're going to head out before Elsa turns into an icicle." She leaned close to fake a whisper to Winnie while still looking at Rainna, "Turns out the cold does get to her, after all."

Rainna giggled at Charlie's silly joke.

"Sounds good. Hopefully West will be done soon and we can head out, too. Text me tomorrow and we'll see if we can get the girls together to play. Bye!"

"Bye!" They exchanged quick side hugs and made their way to the Jeep, waving and chatting with other people they knew on their way.

She saw a paper under the windshield wiper on the Jeep and snatched it off. As she unfolded it, she saw *LEAVE* written on the paper. She looked around and realized she had accidentally parked in front of a fire hydrant. Maybe that was someone's strange way of telling her not to park there. Either that, or someone she knew was joking with her. She crumpled the paper and tossed it into the passenger seat.

Rainna passed out on the short drive home. Charlie carried her in and woke her up to change and brush the candy remnants from her teeth before she fell into bed.

Curling up in Nana's chair, still wearing her costume, she pulled out her phone. Opening her messages, she clicked on one that had arrived a few days before. She hadn't clicked to read it but had looked at the short message preview several times. It felt like the letters all over again. She was afraid of what opening the text would start, so she had put it off.

Malachi Thomas: I talked to the lawyer last week. She said—

Her hand shook a little as she held her phone with her right hand and clicked on the message with her thumb. She had to stop avoiding the things that were hard.

Malachi Thomas: I talked to the lawyer last week. She said it's unlikely to get him a new trial. Something about a case with jurors taking drugs that didn't work out well for the defendant. But she did say if the juror was misusing medications, they weren't upholding their duty. She's going to do some digging, see if it's worth filing anything. Maybe hoping is bad, but I'm still thankful for it.

Charlie let out a shaky breath she hadn't realized she was holding and moved to cradle the phone as she tapped to reply.

Starting and stopping several times, erasing and rewriting, she finally settled for something simple.

Charlie: Thanks for letting me know. Feel free to keep me posted.

She took the tie out of her braid and shook her hair loose as she walked to the table and grabbed the papers in the transcript. It was probably the last thing he intended by talking to her, but her conversation with George had made her want to keep looking. His clear disdain for Darius and his surety that he deserved the death penalty didn't make sense to her. She was jealous of his confidence. Was something making him feel that way, or had he had something against Darius from the beginning? Was Darius right about being a target for being different? For being Black? If she stopped looking now, she would always wonder.

Charlie kept running her conversation with George about the jurors through her mind. Darius's lawyer was talking to jurors. The jurors were then talking to George. The way he described it felt like the jurors thought it was their duty to run everything by George—like he was the boss. But George only represented one side of the case, the state.

Was this evidence that the jurors didn't really weigh the case because they thought their duty was to George and the town? And if so, was it going to be swept under the rug? Was anything else being hidden or ignored?

A part of her wanted to start looking through everything again immediately. But she was tired, frustrated, and felt like she needed to shower. Running into George Marshall made her skin crawl.

Charlie put up the papers, showered, and curled up in bed for the night with her arm wrapped around Buck. Tomorrow she would take a new approach. If something was to be found in the transcript, she had to study it like a class. She would work page by page, objection by objection, and find what she was looking for.

CHAPTER 9

———

Over the next few weeks, Charlie filled her notebook. She broke the transcript down by witness. For each witness, she made a list of their credentials, significant points they made in testimony, objections, and the cause of each objection. She also had color-coded highlights on the document noting interesting quotes or other things that caught her eye.

By the time Charlie made it to the end of the document again, she had come to one major conclusion. If she was on the jury, she would not have voted to convict. There wasn't enough evidence. "Beyond a reasonable doubt" is a high bar, and the prosecution didn't meet it.

The piece de resistance for the prosecution was Darius's DNA. A rape kit was performed during the autopsy, and they found traces of semen matching Darius. Dani had a date with Darius the night she died, and they'd slept together. That didn't seem strange to Charlie. Darius had always admitted that.

The most confusing thing to Charlie was actually the prosecution's theory. The prosecution told the jury that Dani's boyfriend, whom she was sleeping with, got mad at her, raped her, killed her, and then tried to burn the evidence.

Other than the DNA, the prosecution's theory came back to the intimate partner theory. Darius made the most sense as a suspect because he and Dani were intimate. Maybe she tried to break up with him that night. Perhaps he got jealous. Dani was beautiful. Perhaps he suspected she was cheating. She did work at the same hospital as her ex, after all.

There was also the traffic stop, which the prosecution said proved his guilt. But Charlie wondered if it proved the opposite.

In the late night of September 29 or early morning hours of September 30, Darius was pulled over on the outskirts of town for speeding. He was given a verbal warning and he drove home to Oklahoma City.

A neighbor called 911 at 12:28 a.m., saying she saw smoke coming from Dani's house. The fire department arrived at 12:37 a.m. and found Dani unresponsive. The fire was the worst at the front of the house, in the living area. Dani was found in between the main bedroom and bathroom at the back of the house. Dani was pulled from the house, but the process of putting out the fire ruined most of the physical evidence.

There should have been a formal record of the traffic stop with a date and time stamp. But the officer, Harvey Knight, told the court he used his discretion and chose to give Darius a verbal warning. However, he said he looked at the clock on his cruiser when he pulled Darius over, and the time was 12:15 a.m. The stop took place a couple miles from Dani's home.

The prosecution argued that the time, proximity, and being caught "fleeing the scene" proved that Darius did it. Darius's attorney argued that it wasn't possible. They said the traffic stop had to have taken place closer to the time that Darius claimed it took place, 11:30 p.m. The drive takes three hours, and his home alarm showed that he disarmed the system at 2:33 a.m. How could he possibly make a three-hour drive in less than two hours and twenty minutes like the prosecution claimed?

The prosecution argued that he drove fast. The roads were empty at that time of night, so it should be possible.

She kept coming back to another part of the transcript as well. The testimony regarding the fire bothered her. Maybe it was the same thing that had caught Darius's attention. The prosecution used the fire marshal as their expert, a local man in his mid-fifties who had served on the fire department since his early twenties. In addition to his experience with the department, he completed a fire investigation class a few months before the incident. He testified that specific patterns on the floor indicated the fire was intentional—that it had been set on purpose. It was near the front door, probably so the perpetrator could escape.

During the testimony, the defense counsel objected frequently. They claimed the fire marshal's testimony was speculation and not based on science. Charlie remembered that the arson expert the defense put on the stand had looked like a young Rick Moranis. He had a long list of educational credentials and was not shy in criticizing the fire marshal's methods and conclusions. He stated that the fire marshal's report of what happened was based on outdated thinking. It was junk science. From the evidence he was shown regarding the fire, the defense expert found the cause inconclusive.

The defense's theory for the case was that there was no crime. Their theory was that she fell and hit her head, knocking herself unconscious. The candles she'd lit earlier in the night set the curtains on fire. It was a stretch, that two huge accidents could happen one right after another.

It made sense the jury didn't believe that theory. But the arson expert seemed legitimate and he didn't seem to think the fire was intentional. Charlie thought the theory was odd, especially since Darius thought there could be other suspects. But maybe there wasn't any evidence to back up alternative suspect theories, and the defense attorney was allowed to choose their own strategy.

A buzz from Charlie's phone pulled her out of her thoughts.

Winnie: Are we still on for next Friday?

Charlie: Can we order pizza and shop online instead?

Winnie: Stop being a hermit. It's better when you can touch and see stuff. We're going.

Winnie: Tom's watching the kids. He can handle one more. Do you want to drop off Rainna?

Charlie: Sure. Hiding that doll house would be pretty tough if she were with us.

Winnie: Will you make me 2 pies for Thursday? You know mine always suck.

Charlie: Pumpkin and pecan?

Winnie: Did you really ask me that? It's Thanksgiving. I don't want strawberry.

Charlie: Okay, 1 pumpkin and 1 pecan. Anything else?

Winnie: I wish! Tom's mom would judge me if I let you make everything.

One of Charlie's sponsors had reached out earlier about making sure her post would be live in time for Thanksgiving shopping and prep. Charlie hadn't even started it. Two other posts needed to be done before the holiday, too. The high school Family and Consumer Science teacher had also talked her into teaching a class and talking to the students about her blog, so she was trying to schedule a day that worked. She groaned thinking about how crazy her next few days would be when her phone buzzed again.

Winnie: Ethan's going to be happy to get your pie ;)
Charlie: I'll drop your pies off Wednesday.
Winnie: Crap, Sarah's out of bed. That kid is sneaky and she likes to pop up in places like a ghost. Luckily her door squeaks. Love you! Gotta go.
Charlie: Good luck getting your wraith back to sleep. Night!

Charlie sighed. No matter how many times Charlie told Winnie that it wouldn't happen with Ethan, she just couldn't give up. Maybe it was because Winnie, more than anyone, knew how much Charlie had once loved Ethan. He helped her heal after her mother had died. He was there when she was a teenager whose older sister was away at college and whose father had checked out.

But she and Ethan weren't the same people they had been in high school. Winnie still saw Charlie like she used to be—someone who went with the flow. Maybe that's why Charlie still loved being around Winnie so much. She was reminded of a time when life was simpler.

Charlie ran her hand through her hair, stood up, and stretched. It was after ten, and she'd been sitting and reading since Rainna went to bed around eight. Charlie gathered the stack of papers and notes and put them away. Rainna didn't need to see what Charlie was reading. She would see her mom's name and ask about it like she had done with the letter.

Her phone buzzed again, and she reached for it thinking that it was still Winnie.

Malachi Thomas: Lawyer's not going to file anything. At least not right now. Wanted you to know. I'm still grateful that you passed the information along.

Her eyebrows drew together, and she pursed her lips. As the realization that she was no longer confident Darius had committed the murder became more apparent to her, she had hoped the issue with the juror would be enough to help him fix this. Maybe a new trial would flesh out all of the evidence that was missing. Was the lawyer looking for something else, or was this an acknowledgment that this wasn't a battle they could win?

She had exchanged a few messages with Malachi over the last few weeks. They were related to the trial, like, "why did the lawyer use that arson guy as their expert?" and "what did you think of the defense theory?" and his opinions on witnesses. He always answered. Quickly.

Her phone vibrated in her hand. She glanced at it and giggled.

Malachi Thomas: What's chocolate gravy, and why would you write about it? I'm doubting your culinary skills. You're a fraud, aren't you?

Charlie: I'm a woman who loves food. I've never claimed to be anything else. Shame on you for disparaging chocolate gravy. It's life changing. There's a reason it's one of my most popular posts.

Malachi Thomas: I guess I'll have to try it someday...

She was tempted to tell him that she was no longer sure Darius had done it. That she wouldn't have voted to convict him.

But she hesitated. Once she opened that door, could she ever go back?

As she crawled in between the covers, turned out the light, and made room for Buck on the bed, she smiled at the thought of Malachi Thomas trying chocolate gravy.

CHAPTER 10

———

Charlie and Rainna made it to Winnie's house the morning after Thanksgiving just as the sun was coming up and illuminating the fog on the quiet country road.

"Perfect timing!" Winnie said answering the door for them. When they arrived, Winnie's house was a flurry of activity, and Rainna jumped right in, grabbing breakfast as she kissed Charlie goodbye. "See you, Auntie! You better buy me a dream house!"

"Dream house, what's a dream house?" she teased. With a tug of Rainna's braid and a quick kiss, she left her in the capable hands of Winnie's family.

"Your pies were delicious, as always," Winnie said as she and Charlie got into Winnie's Yukon. "Even if you didn't make the ones with chocolate crust. I saw all the buzz those were getting on social media."

"I'm sorry I've treated my best friend so poorly, but I'm glad you liked the pies anyway."

"So, how did yesterday go?" Winnie asked.

"Ugh, I know it makes me a total grinch, but I'm not into family Thanksgivings," Charlie said, remembering the day before with her aunt and uncle, Betti and her kids, and Betti's brother, Owen. Her aunt had insisted that Charlie and Rainna come over. Charlie had weaseled out of it the last few years but couldn't think of a good excuse this year.

"Oh hush, you're probably just mad that you had to eat someone else's cooking and pretend that it's just as good as yours." Winnie laughed.

"The cranberry sauce was from a can. She sliced it and it looked like mini coasters. Making cranberry sauce from scratch takes, like, ten minutes!" Charlie said.

"You're such a snob," Winnie teased. "Okay, ignore the food. How was the rest of it?"

"Parts of it were good. I hadn't seen Owen in over a year, so I was glad he drove in. We've always gotten along. Sounds like he finally has a girlfriend. She's divorced with two kids. He's smitten. Showed me a ton of pictures of all of them together."

"So Owen was the good part. What were the bad parts?"

Charlie glanced at Winnie. "Aunt Penny heard I requested the trial transcript. I was grilled for thirty minutes about why I would want to put myself through reading about my own sister's death. She asked if I had some sort of murder fetish. The whole time, Uncle Arnie was sitting next to her watching football and pretending like he couldn't hear the conversation. Also, as much as I love Uncle Arnie, he looks so much like dad, that it makes me angry and sad all at the same time."

Charlie shook her head and tucked her legs underneath her in the passenger seat. "As if that all wasn't enough, she started talking about how I only had a few child-bearing years left. That no men were going to want me anymore if I couldn't give them babies. She asked if I wanted to die alone with only a dog for company. I may or may not have said yes." Charlie smirked remembering the look of horror on her aunt's face. "All the while, everyone pretended that everything was perfectly normal with Betti and Mike. Even though he wasn't there and when I asked, Uncle Arnie gave me the wide-eyed head shake that meant 'leave it alone.'"

Laughter filled the car as Winnie tried to wring more details of the holiday's awkwardness from Charlie.

"Aunt Penny also said something weird about dad's girlfriend. But when I said that dad didn't have a girlfriend, she ran into the kitchen saying that she could smell the bread burning. I tried to ask her about it later, but she found another reason to leave the room."

Winnie shook her head. "I never heard that your dad had a girlfriend, but that doesn't mean anything. After all these years, he was bound to have a few secrets."

Charlie thought about her dad and how little she knew about his life. He was the type of person to have many secrets.

They spent the next several hours hopping from one big box store to the next. Winnie caught Charlie up on all the cases she'd transcribed lately. She gave Charlie some hilarious details about jurors answering questions with a little too much honesty, like telling the story of their conception between their father, their mother's best friend, and a turkey baster.

"Ethan says he hasn't seen you around town lately," Winnie looked at Charlie out of the side of her eye.

Charlie ignored the part about Ethan and said she'd been spending most of her time at home. "Oh, I forgot to tell you, I did have an interesting interaction at the feed store when I was picking up stuff for Buck the other day."

"Oh yeah?"

Charlie turned to face Winnie in the driver's seat. "So I ran into the old coach from school, the one who taught girls basketball. I tried to say hi to him and he refused to talk to me. Wouldn't even look at me. When I finally walked away, I heard him call me trash."

"Mr. Cartwright?" Winnie asked, looking like she was trying to hold in a laugh. "You know he was always a little off. Told me I was going to end up with a baby before I graduated high school 'cause I wore my shirts too low." Winnie glanced down at her generous top and burst out laughing. "Okay, well, maybe he wasn't too far off on that one. But he probably didn't even remember who you were, and I'm pretty sure he calls everybody trash."

They were laughing as Winnie continued with more ridiculous stories from the courthouse. Her driving made Charlie nervous with her expressive gesturing and constant looking at herself in the rearview mirror while driving. Winnie had always been a bad driver, but Charlie rode with her so rarely that she forgot until it was too late.

The conversation lulled and Charlie was fried from so much human interaction that her eyes drifted shut. Her head was resting on the window when Winnie's voice snapped her back to the present.

"Oh my goodness, have I told you about Tom's client? He allegedly," Winnie used air quotes around the word, keeping her hands off the wheel for longer than Charlie was comfortable with, "took a little boy from a playground! Luckily, he didn't even make it past the parking lot. Could you imagine how terrified his mother must have been?"

"That's horrifying." She shifted so she could wrap her arms around her legs and rest her head on her knees. "I'm no longer taking my eyes off of Rainna for even a second. Isn't it supposed to be safe around here? That's one of the reasons I stay."

"I know! Just imagine how it feels to have multiple kids at the playground and realizing you can't watch them all at the same time. But most of the time, everyone looks out for each other."

"So what was up with the guy? Why was he trying to take the little boy? Do you know, or can you not tell me?"

"Well, that's actually the only reason Tom took the case. This guy's been his client before. Tom says he's super nice and actually a good guy. But he's got some kind of issue, and when his meds aren't right, or he's not taking them, he gets bizarre ideas. Like with this one," Winnie said shaking her head. "He swears the little boy is his."

"Did he have something going on with the mom?"

"Nope. She swears she's never met the guy."

Charlie pushed her hair behind her ears. "Then why would he think the kid is his?"

"Well, I guess several years ago, hopefully before he started having these issues, that is if it's true at all, he said he was a sperm donor. He said the kid looked exactly like he did at that age, and he just knew. He believed the kid was his and thought he had every right to take his," Winnie used air quotes again, "little boy home."

Charlie's shoulders jerked involuntarily like a cold chill was running down her spine. "Whoa."

"The kid's dad stopped it. He'd gone to grab something out of the car when he heard his wife scream. He beat the guy bloody until someone pulled him off."

"That's crazy. Where did this happen? Why haven't I heard anything about it?" Charlie asked.

"It happened at the big playground over by the park. Not very many people know about it yet because the mom's the newspaper editor's niece. She was embarrassed and asked him not to run it yet. He held off for her. But if it ends up going to trial instead of pleading out, there's no way that they can keep it under wraps."

Charlie rested her chin in her hand, trying to figure out the best way to ask the question lingering in her mind. "So, this client, is he in jail now?"

"Nope, he's in the mental health facility. Tom convinced the judge to release him to the facility so they could get his meds back on track before trial."

"Does Tom go over there to see him?"

"Yeah, I think he's got an appointment over there next week. Why?" Winnie gave her a suspicious look, and Charlie knew she had failed at subtlety.

"The story reminds me of something that someone told me about Dani and Rainna. It's probably nothing, might not even be the same guy, but it makes me wonder." She tapped her index finger on her lip.

Charlie didn't love admitting her theories or what she was looking into. But she was sick of hiding it from everyone. She didn't have to tell Winnie about Darius's letter and that he was the one who told her the story of Dani's patient. Still, she wasn't going to lie to Winnie, either.

Winnie studied her. "Well, he's been around here for a while. Makes sense that Dani would've crossed paths with him at the hospital. Talk to Tom."

They dropped Charlie's purchases off at her house on the way back to Winnie's to keep Rainna from seeing anything.

"Tom texted me that he ordered pizza while we were at your place. You and Rainna have to stay for dinner," Winnie said to Charlie, keeping her gaze on the road instead of looking at Charlie like she normally would.

Charlie noticed a shift in how Winnie was acting, but pizza was pizza. "Yes, ma'am. I don't say no to pizza."

Gravel crunched under the tires as they drove up to Winnie's, and Charlie noticed an extra car in the drive. She heard a shriek and looked to the side of the house where there was a game of touch football. Tom was running around with his kids and Rainna was riding on Ethan's back.

"Thanks for the setup, Win. I guess I walked right into that one. The pizza better be delicious 'cause you owe me." Charlie shook her head, torn between wanting to laugh at Winnie's guilty look and being annoyed that, once again, her best friend had put her in an awkward situation.

Rainna slid off Ethan's back and ran full blast into Charlie's legs. "Auntie! Did you buy me a dream house?"

"I have no clue what you're talking about." Charlie lifted her brows and looked down at Rainna.

"Come on, Auntie! Tell me!" Rainna was bouncing on the balls of her feet.

"Give your aunt a break, little one. Go, play." Ethan gave Rainna a gentle shove back toward the action of the game in the yard. Charlie felt a spike of irritation at him insinuating himself into their family moment. Ethan pushed his hands in his pockets, looking sheepish. "When Tom invited me over tonight, he didn't say anything about you being here. But I guessed it when I saw little miss. Sorry to surprise you."

"It's fine," Charlie replied. "I'm sorry about the night you were over for dinner. I was in a weird mood. You cool if we just forget it?"

Ethan shrugged, never one to hold a grudge. "Let's grab some food."

They headed inside and stuffed themselves with pizza. Winnie set it up where Ethan and Charlie were sitting next to one another throughout the meal. They didn't exchange more than a few words, but Charlie felt on edge. Each time their thighs brushed beneath the table or they reached for something at the same time, it made it worse. By the time she finished her meal, she was ready to get back to the quiet of the house with only Rainna.

Charlie stood to let her hosts know she would be heading out when Ethan's voice boomed beside her, "Little miss! How about I take you and your aunt out for ice cream?"

Rainna was wiggling in her seat, looking at Charlie. "Can I have chocolate brownie? In a cone?"

Charlie worked hard to keep her annoyance at Ethan for putting her on the spot from showing. Keeping her attention on her niece, she replied, "Of course, sweets. But let's get going because it's getting late. Ethan, we'll meet you there. Winnie, thanks for a fun day. See y'all later! Bye!" She threw a glare at Winnie and headed toward the door to make her escape when she remembered what Winnie had told her about Tom's client.

"Hey, Tom, I've got a question for you. Is it alright if I give you a call on Monday?"

Tom's face showed surprise at her request. "Of course! I've got meetings in the afternoon, but I'm free in the morning." As Charlie was walking out the door, she saw Tom looking askance at Winnie. She was pretty sure Winnie would tell him all about their conversation. A twinge of guilt took up space in her already full belly, but she knew Winnie could hold her own. It wasn't the first time Winnie had talked about Tom's clients, and it wouldn't be the last.

The door slammed behind Charlie and Rainna, but she heard the hinges squeak again before she could make it to the Jeep. Ethan was close behind. She buckled Rainna into her car seat and hopped into the driver's seat without so much as a glance at him.

Charlie hated that he found ways to trap her into spending time with him. Rainna had fun with Ethan, and he took advantage of that. Ethan knew that if he asked Rainna, Charlie wouldn't be able to say no. A part of her also hated that Ethan was so good with Rainna. Other people didn't understand why she didn't want to be with him. But Charlie had never appreciated other people forcing her into things, even when they thought it was for her own good. Ethan was the kind of guy who thought he knew what was best. And he thought he was best for Charlie.

Well, if she was forced to spend more time with him, she would at least try to get something out of it. The transcript had answered some of her questions, but she had more. And the police file might hold some of the pieces she was looking for. Since it was no longer an active case, maybe she could talk Ethan into giving it to her, the same way he had talked her into ice cream.

CHAPTER 11

———

The bell over the door jingled and the smell of waffle cones and coffee hit Charlie as they entered the shop. Ethan was waiting at the counter with a big smile showing his dimple on the right. Like many other small-town businesses, the ice cream shop was one of three businesses inside the storefront. It also served as a coffee shop in the mornings and a boutique that sold clothes and knickknacks. They made their way over to the display case to look at the different flavors.

"Little Miss, what's your favorite flavor? I'm a pralines and cream guy, but I'm guessing you're more of a cotton candy or bubblegum girl. Am I right?" Ethan had knelt to Rainna's level. Charlie tried to keep herself from rolling her eyes. Rainna had already told them what she wanted at Winnie's, but Ethan must not have paid attention. Tucking her hands in her pockets to warm her cold fingers, she watched the two of them.

Rainna wrinkled her nose. "Cotton candy's okay, I guess. My favorite's chocolate brownie. It's so chocolatey! It tastes like Auntie's brownies covered in chocolate ice cream." Rainna's "r" in ice cream came out with a "w" sound—a sweet reminder to Charlie that Rainna was still a baby in some ways, even if she felt grown up in others.

Charlie ordered strawberry in a cup for herself and Rainna's chocolate brownie in a cone. "How much for mine and hers?" Charlie asked the clerk while pointing to Rainna. The clerk ignored her and looked to Ethan.

"Come on, Char. I'm not going to make you pay for your own ice cream." He handed his card to the clerk and then stuffed some ones in the tip jar. A slight growl of annoyance made its way out of Charlie, both at the clerk for ignoring her and at Ethan.

Ethan and Rainna were already seated at a booth by the time Charlie got her order. They were sitting on opposite sides, and he scooted over to let Charlie sit beside him. She took her place next to Rainna in the hard booth, pretending she didn't see his invitation.

They spent several minutes eating and listening to Rainna chatter about her day with Winnie's kids. One of them must have used the word "butt" because Rainna couldn't stop repeating it and laughing like it was the funniest thing in the world. Rainna was bright, but she still had the sense of humor of a little kid.

When Rainna finished, she made her way over to a corner with toys. She stacked and played with the red and black pieces of checkers.

Charlie watched Rainna, and when she felt Ethan's gaze on her, she looked him in the eye. Ethan reached over and touched her arm. "I'm sorry if it seemed like I was annoyed when you asked about Lanie. I told you I was there to answer your questions, but I didn't. The thing is, what Lanie's dealing with now has nothing to do with back then. I could have just told you that I couldn't answer that one. I get that your concern all comes back to Dani. Sorry."

She reached over and gave his hand on her arm a quick pat. She meant the gesture to thank him but also to let him know that he didn't need to keep his hand on her. "I'm sorry, too. Like I said before, I was in a weird mood."

"You're allowed to miss Dani. You're allowed to grieve. You don't have to be perfect, you know." They had spent so much time together after her mom passed away when Charlie was in high school that he knew her grief well. Her mother had always made her feel loved and wanted. She and Charlie had baked together, and before she got sick, she would go running with Charlie to help her with track.

Her mother had helped to smooth her dad's rough edges. He had said mean things even when Charlie's mother was alive—like when he would tell people that Charlie was nothing but an accident—but at least in those days he would show up to track meets and awards assemblies. Charlie's father had always acted like he didn't care about what anyone thought, with the exception of her mother.

When her mom died, she had tried to be the perfect daughter, making perfect grades and homemade meals for her dad. But even that wasn't enough to please him. Charlie wondered if things would have been better if Dani hadn't already moved out and gone to college when their mother had died.

Now, with Dani's death, she had fallen into the perfection trap again. She was trying to be the perfect aunt, raising Rainna the way she thought Dani would have wanted—in the small town that Dani loved surrounded by people who had known Dani and could tell Rainna stories about her mother as she got older.

"I just feel like I don't have a good grasp on anything. Some things just don't make sense to me. I have doubts." Charlie reached back to rub her neck where she felt a tension headache building. She knew Ethan believed Darius had done it. And if he believed something, he completely believed it. He was unshakeable.

"Here, let me do that," Ethan quickly moved from his side of the booth to Charlie's and started rubbing her neck before she knew what was happening. She straightened and put as much distance between them as she could while trapped on the inside of the booth.

"I've got it," Charlie told him. "Do you mind heading back to the other side?" she raised her eyebrows and tilted her head toward the recently vacated seat. "It's easier for me to see you while we talk."

A look of annoyance crossed Ethan's face, but he moved back to his side.

"Now, this has nothing do to with the investigation, and I'm not sure what Dani told you about him," Ethan said when he was settled on his side. "But I saw them out together a time or two in town—her and Darius. I wasn't impressed. He was like a peacock strutting around in his fancy clothes. All shine, no substance. I even saw her paying for their dinner once. What kind of man lets a woman pay for their meal?" Ethan shook his head, offended at the idea that a woman could want to pay or that a man would allow her to do so. That belief was yet another reason that Charlie knew they were no longer compatible.

"Auntie, look!" Rainna pointed at a tower she had built out of the checkers and some random blocks in the play area.

"That's great, sweets! Can you make it even taller?" Charlie liked to encourage Rainna to think bigger and keep trying, even on small tasks. Rainna went back to building and Charlie tried to get the conversation on better footing so she could make her request.

"Everything at work okay? Do you still like being the man in charge?" she asked.

"Yep." He nodded his head. "You know me. I always wanted to be a cop. I love that I get to do this every day. Our town's never been safer." He talked about some of the staffing changes in his department, one guy getting promoted and finding a new receptionist when the last quit after she had her baby.

Charlie tried to pay attention but found her gaze wandering to the clerk behind the counter. The clerk was talking animatedly on her phone, glancing at her and Ethan every so often. Charlie could hear a little of what she was saying, "so damn hot... use his handcuffs." Charlie was trying to keep from chuckling out loud and giving herself away to Ethan that she wasn't paying attention when she heard, "stuck up... thinks she's too good." Charlie sat up straighter, pretty sure she had just been insulted by the twenty-something behind the counter.

"Ethan," she looked away from the rude clerk, "how does your office handle public access requests? I was wondering if I could get a copy of the police report from Dani's investigation?" Charlie decided to ask outright rather than beat around the bush.

"The police report?" A look of confusion crossed Ethan's face. Charlie couldn't be sure whether it was from the change of subject or the request.

"Yeah. It's a closed case. Right? Darius is in prison. His appeals are done. You would know better than I do, but I think I can formally request it through the Freedom of

Information Act. Does your department require me to come in and file a request?"

When she'd finished the transcript, she had looked up how to get a police report for a closed case. She should be able to get a copy by filing a request, but each department was different. She had read some horror stories about departments claiming a case was still active so they didn't have to share the report.

"Why do you want it?" Ethan asked, scratching his head and looking at her suspiciously.

"I have questions. You know me. I need to see things with my own eyes to believe them. Maybe if I see the investigation with my own eyes, it'll make sense." The last sentence was a stretch, but she didn't feel bad about the exaggeration. She did have to see things with her own eyes to believe them. But the more she thought about the case over the last few weeks, the more she realized she didn't think the evidence existed that would make her believe Darius did it. At least not in the police file. Otherwise, there would have been more presented at the trial. Each day, her doubts that he could have done it had grown.

Rather than keep pushing, Charlie decided to let him sit with the request. She hoped that by making her request directly to him she wouldn't have to go through the official process. The fewer people who knew what she was doing, the better. And this way might be faster.

Ethan reached over and grabbed Charlie's hand.

"Charlie, I can't imagine how difficult all this has been for you. I'm sorry you feel like you've still got questions. But, babe, he did it."

Charlie counted to five, trying to temper her annoyance at the pet name. It wasn't a term of endearment she liked, but she hated it even more that he felt entitled to use it. She took a deep breath to steel herself for what she would say next.

"Ethan," she said as she removed her hand from his, "you're a good friend. And Rainna loves you, but I'm not looking for anything. I like being on my own." Charlie felt awkward bringing this up out of the blue when he hadn't mentioned anything about dating. Still, he had trapped her into this outing and kept touching her, so she felt justified.

Ethan leaned across the table on his forearms, bringing his upper body closer to hers. With an earnest look on his face he said, "You don't mean that. Nobody really wants to be alone. I'm not sure what happened with you and that guy from law school, but don't let him ruin the rest of your life. I know it's been a long time, but you and I were great together. We can be again. I don't understand why you're being so stubborn."

Sincerity shone in his eyes as he looked at her, which made it harder, but she was sick of this. She reached out to pat his hand. She wanted him to understand that she meant what she said. She thought the extra point of contact would help him focus on her words. "Ethan, you're right. We were great. Once. A very long time ago. But even that crashed and burned. I'm a very different person than I was back then. You and I don't want the same things."

A look of hurt flashed across his eyes. He took the hand that she had rested on his and tried to thread their fingers together, but she pulled back. He ran his hand over his head. Anyone else would have had mussed hair, but he kept his so short that it stayed the same.

"Okay, I hear you. You've changed. I get that, Charlie. I do. I've changed, too. A guy can't go into the military and come out the same as when he went in. We're both different people.

Don't you think it's unfair for you to prejudge what you think I want? Can't we just try it out and see where things go?"

Charlie stifled a sigh of frustration. She was divorced, in her thirties, and raising a child. Couldn't she make her own decisions? Why did people always have to act like they knew better than she did? She also didn't get why Ethan, and everyone else, seemed to want them back together.

Charlie tried to avoid Ethan's stare only to see that Rainna had grown bored with the blocks and checkers. Rainna was climbing onto the chairs. Charlie stood and moved toward her. "Rainna, please climb down from that chair right now, sweets."

"I better take her home. It's been a long day. She got up early, and I'm guessing she didn't get her usual nap at Winnie and Tom's. Thanks for the ice cream, Ethan." Charlie grabbed the trash off the table and threw away her cup. She walked over and picked Rainna up, setting her on her hip. Rainna was getting too big to carry, but Charlie couldn't bring herself to stop.

Ethan made his way over to them. "Let me take her."

Charlie was about to tell him that she had it when Rainna lunged for Ethan. They made their way out to the Jeep. Rainna gave Ethan a hug, and he promised to visit her soon. Charlie started the Jeep so it could warm up while Ethan buckled Rainna into her car seat.

"I want to talk to you about this more," Ethan told Charlie.

Charlie shut the driver's door so Rainna wouldn't overhear their conversation. She felt her phone in her back pocket vibrate, usually an indication that she had a text message.

"I've gotta get Rainna in bed." Charlie pointed to the back seat of the Jeep, where Rainna had already passed out with her head leaning forward in her car seat. "Let me know how I need to go about getting the police report."

Ethan was scratching his chin. Stubble from a long day was starting to appear. "I'll think about it. But I don't like you spending your time this way. And I want to continue the other conversation we were having. Soon."

Without answering, Charlie shook her head and climbed into the driver's seat. When he turned to walk to his vehicle, she pulled her phone out of her back pocket.

Malachi: I hope you had a happy Thanksgiving

A smile touched Charlie's lips.

Charlie: If I never see another pumpkin pie, it will be too soon.
Charlie: Scratch that. I'm talking crazy. Pumpkin pie is fantastic, and I'll be making it again by Christmas.

Charlie was starting to look forward to Malachi's texts. They never really said too much to one another, but it was nice to talk to someone different. She had let a lot of relationships with her law school friends drop when she got divorced.

Breaking up was awkward enough without sharing friends. It made more sense for him to keep their law school friends, anyway, as he's the one who stayed.

Now, the main people she talked to were from her hometown, which she found ironic, as she had always been so eager to leave. But since she had called Malachi, it was like she had a line to the outside world again. It was a complicated and messy line, disturbed by a lot of static. But it was nice to have.

Most people wouldn't understand why she was communicating with the brother of the man who was convicted of killing her sister. But since Dani had died, Charlie had felt so alone. She had lost her favorite person, the one she turned to when she needed someone to make her feel understood. Charlie loved Winnie, but Winnie had never fully understood Charlie, as much as she tried. Their lives were too different. Charlie had lived through loss and disappointment in ways Winnie couldn't grasp.

From the beginning of her conversations with Malachi, she felt a kinship with him. While it wasn't the same kind as hers, Malachi understood loss and disappointment. He had lost his brother, even if Darius was still alive. And the entire experience with Darius had disappointed Malachi in ways that even Charlie could not comprehend.

Charlie: How was your holiday?

She didn't want to wait in the parking lot on his reply, so she pushed her phone under her leg, and reversed out of her spot. The thought of another text gave her something to look forward to as she shivered in her Jeep all the way home.

CHAPTER 12

———

Charlie reached for the remote to turn off the television. The national morning news program was over, leaving the local hosts talking about a crash that took place overnight on the major highway. Charlie grabbed her phone, turning it over a few times in her hands before setting it down. She shook out her hands, grabbed it again, and dialed Tom. She had already dropped Rainna off for the day and wanted to talk to Tom before she started playing around with a new recipe.

She'd learned the hard way that it was too easy to miss putting ingredients in when she was distracted. In the past, it had resulted in a cake that didn't rise because she left out the baking powder and chocolate chip cookies without the chocolate chips. She was still embarrassed to remember pulling the cookies out of the oven, only to realize that she had left out the thing that made them special. And she was definitely distracted today. She couldn't stop wondering if Tom's client had anything to do with Dani's death.

After four rings, she heard Tom's deep voice, "Howard Law Office. What can I do for you?"

"Picking up your own phone today?" Charlie asked.

"Hey, Charlie. Nancy's running late. Something about an unbalanced washing machine. How's it going?"

Instead of sounding annoyed, like Charlie thought most lawyers would if they had to handle the phones, Tom seemed to find the situation with his legal secretary funny. Charlie had always admired how good-humored he was. She assumed his easy disposition was one of the things that had drawn Winnie to him.

"Did Winnie tell you why I wanted to talk?" Winnie and Tom shared everything. Charlie had no doubt that as soon as the kids were in bed the night she'd been over there, Winnie had spilled their conversation.

"She said she mentioned my client and the boy. Don't worry. I didn't tell her anything that was privileged. She could have, and would have, found it out elsewhere. She also said you thought he may have had some connection with Dani. Is that right?"

"Yeah." She let out a big breath. "So, I'm asking that you please don't tell Winnie everything that I'm going to say. Can you do that?" Charlie wasn't ready for everything to get back to Winnie, Ethan, or anyone else. Tom meant well, but she was also one hundred percent sure he told his wife client confidences, whether he would admit it or not.

The line was silent for a moment while Tom seemed to be weighing his decision. "Alright. I'll just tell Winnie the bare bones. If we need to tell her more, you and I can figure out what to tell her together. But she'd kill me if she just thought I was keeping secrets from her, so there's gotta be a better reason. Drop by and give me five bucks, and then I'll be your lawyer. That way our conversations will be privileged."

Charlie chuckled at Tom's reasoning, "Tom, you already are my lawyer. My dad's estate—remember? And I know I'm not the one who finished law school, but I'm pretty sure that's not exactly how that works. But whatever. Fine. I'll give you five bucks, and this can be confidential."

"Okay then, shoot," Tom told her.

Charlie could feel her heartbeat speed up. "I want to meet him—your client. But I need to be upfront with you about why. I'd like you to ask him if I can come by. Of course, I want you to be there—"

Tom cut her off, "Slow down, Charlie. You're rambling. Just tell me what's going on."

"So... somebody told me that when Dani was alive, this guy was a patient in the ER. He thought that Rainna was his. I don't know all the details. They said the guy found out Dani's baby was born through a surrogate with Dani's eggs and a donor's sperm. This patient claimed he was a sperm donor, so he immediately thought Rainna was his. I know it sounds ridiculous and a little crazy. But when Winnie told me the story about this guy saying he thought a random kid was his, I don't know. I just, I guess something about it was weird. I wanted to meet him." She took a big breath.

She had tried to get everything out quickly, and she had so many strange emotions—uncertainty, embarrassment, fear, hope—running through her. Her hands were shaking. She could feel the sweat under her arms and at the small of her back. Buck pushed his nose into her hand, his way of getting her to pet him.

When she first had the idea of meeting Tom's client, it felt like a logical next step. But asking Tom about it made the whole situation feel surreal. She was also starting to see the flaw in the logic. Tom's client probably wasn't even the patient from the ER. And just because the patient thought he was Rainna's father didn't mean he had a reason to kill

Dani. Did he even know where she had lived? The night Dani died, Rainna wasn't even there. Charlie scratched Buck's ears absentmindedly. *This sounds crazy.*

"There's something you're leaving out, Charlie. You're not the kind of person to go chasing rumors that don't mean anything. Why do you think this is important?" She knew Tom would see through any subterfuge, which is why she hadn't lied. Not that she was the type to lie about something like this, anyway.

"I'm not sure Darius did it," Charlie admitted, pinching her bottom lip between her thumb and forefinger. "I don't really think this guy did it, either. Honest. But I was already looking into things when Winnie mentioned it. Someone had floated the idea of this patient who thought he was Rainna's father as a suspect. I thought it was worth trying to meet him. Maybe he knows something. I don't know, Tom. I feel like I've been letting everything happen to me, and maybe I just want to do something, to feel like I've got a little bit of control in my life."

A part of her was afraid that Tom would shut her down immediately.

"What makes you think Darius didn't do it?" His voice was calm and steady, but something about the way he asked the question made her think the answer was important to him.

"I've been through the transcript," Charlie told him. She was still hesitant for anyone to know about the letters from Darius or her communications with Malachi. "The prosecution didn't meet their burden. And if there was more evidence, wouldn't they have presented it? It seems like the jury convicted him because he was the only option they were given."

Tom was silent so long that she checked her phone to make sure the call hadn't dropped. "Don't tell Winnie I said this. Ever. Or Ethan. But I agree. There wasn't enough evidence." He let out a long sigh. "Look, I tell you what, I'll call him and see if you can come with me the next time I stop by to see him. You can't upset him or try to push him. You do, and you leave. Also, if you ask him anything I don't like, you're gone before he can answer."

"Deal," Charlie said quickly before Tom could change his mind. Her leg started bouncing as an outlet for the excitement from her tiny win.

"I'm only agreeing because I think there's no way he did this. I'll even see what I can do to track his movements from back then. I get that this is a door you need to shut. I'll try to help you. Don't make me regret it." He sounded like he did when he got onto his kids for misbehaving.

"Yes, sir." Charlie saluted, even though he couldn't see her. "But seriously, thanks. I'll drop the five bucks by soon so you can keep your trap shut. I appreciate it. I'll let you go so you can get back to saving the world. Text me when you hear back from him about visiting."

"Bye, Charlie. Be good."

Tom liked to tell Charlie to be good. He said the same thing to his kids. It always made her wonder if he saw her as a kid. Or maybe Winnie had embellished their youth to the point that he thought she still needed the admonishment. Either way, she liked it. Something about being told to be good made her feel youthful and like maybe she should find a way to not be so good.

Charlie smiled as she headed toward the pantry to pull out ingredients. She felt like she'd already had one win today and was hoping for another win in the kitchen.

The next morning, Charlie was covered in flour and powdered sugar. The house smelled like chocolate from the cake in the oven. She was singing Alanis Morrissette's "You Oughta Know" and dancing with Buck's paws on her hips with his nails digging into her skin, waiting for the timer. The music stopped briefly, and her phone showed a new text.

> **Tom:** I have a meeting with Martin on Thursday at 10. You can meet me there.
> **Charlie:** See you soon!

Charlie felt a fluttering of nerves at the thought of meeting the guy. She tried to prepare for the meeting, but she felt like she was at a loss for where to start. She didn't even know the guy's name. Based on Tom's text, she assumed his first name was Martin, but maybe that was his last name. She had gone to school with a guy named Nesbit Johnson. He chose to go by Johnson because he said Nesbit was lame. Personally, she thought Johnson would be tougher to go by, but you never knew.

Between work and playing with Rainna, Charlie tried to find him online. She used Martin as a reference looking through local criminal cases since Winnie mentioned he had been Tom's client before. She found one guy with Martin as his last name who had a couple DUIs and then two guys with Martin as a first name. One with a record of physical violence—assault and battery, domestic violence, and assault with a deadly weapon. The other guy had a couple of charges related to harassment.

Charlie wasn't sure which of the three Martins she was hoping to meet. If it was the assault Martin, he could be a decent suspect for a murder. But Tom seemed to like him, and she had a hard time believing Tom would like someone with a violent past. Charlie's best guess was harassment Martin.

On Thursday morning, after dropping Rainna off at school and going for a run in the misty morning air with Buck's tail hitting her leg as they ran, Charlie got dressed to meet Tom and Martin. She spent several minutes staring at her clothing options. What did one wear to meet someone who could be a suspect in their sister's murder? She only had a few choices of business dress, but she didn't want to come off like a lawyer. She was also starting to associate all those clothes with funerals—Nana's, Dani's, her father's.

Martin may be more likely to talk to her if she looked like a regular person. Did that mean that she should wear her everyday uniform of TOMS and a fitted tee, or was it more of a boots and sweater type of conversation?

Charlie settled on boots and a sweater, ran a brush through her long dark hair, put on mascara, and headed out the door. The steering wheel was cold under her hands. The Jeep probably wouldn't be warm until she was already at her destination.

The Russell Memorial Medical Health Center was located on the opposite end of town from her house. It was a run-down red brick building. She had been inside a few times when she was in high school. Winnie and Ethan's grandmother had suffered from Alzheimer's. She had stayed there briefly before their family could get her a spot in a better facility further away.

Charlie parked and spent a few minutes trying to memorize her questions. She hated the idea of freezing up and wasting any opportunity.

When the clock on her dash read 9:58, Charlie hopped out and headed inside. As she pushed open the heavy glass door, her nose was assaulted by a mixture of bleach and a smell that reminded her of the locker room in a high school gymnasium.

She told the woman at the front desk that she was meeting Tom Howard for a visit with Martin. Tom's car was in the lot, so she knew he was here already.

Another staff member led her down a long hall with white vinyl tile. They passed several open doors to rooms with occupants lying on their beds or sitting and watching television. Nurses accompanied some, and many openly stared as she walked past. When they were almost at the end of the hall, the escort reached up and knocked at a door on the right. There was a plate on the door with the name Martin Flanagan. *Harassment Martin.*

The door was pulled wide, and Tom stood with a smile. His salt-and-pepper hair was combed over and his Donald Duck tie was crooked. "Charlie, right on time."

Behind Tom, sitting on the edge of a twin-size mattress with a brown comforter, was a thin man who looked to be in his mid-to-late-fifties. The room was tidy but felt dirty with the old stained floors and ratty furniture. Martin had hair the color of autumn leaves that lay haphazardly across his narrow forehead. The red hair caught her off guard, and she almost giggled at the absurdity of the situation.

One look at Rainna, and anyone would know that her biological father was not the man sitting on the bed in front of Charlie. Charlie never saw the paperwork for the sperm donor that Dani chose, but she did know a few things about the guy. First, he wasn't from around this area. Second, he had an MBA. And third, while he had been born in the United States, his family was from Mexico.

"Martin? Hi, I'm Charlie. Thanks for letting me come down here to meet you."

He immediately rose to his feet, and Charlie noticed he was a tall man, probably six feet since he had at least a couple of inches on her. He reached for her hand. His was clammy, bony, and had the soft quality of a man who didn't work with his hands.

Looking into his warm brown eyes, she was startled by the eagerness she saw. He appeared joyful to have a visitor. She glanced over at Tom and he smirked.

When Tom didn't jump in and say anything, Charlie took the lead. She motioned for Martin to return to his seat, and she took the chair she assumed Tom had vacated when she came in the door. The chair made an awkward sound as she adjusted herself on the vinyl. Tom was leaning against the wall, watching.

Charlie wiped her palms on her pants, trying to get rid of the damp feeling. She didn't know if the clamminess was due to shaking Martin's hand or because her own palms were sweating.

"Martin, did Tom tell you why I wanted to meet with you?"

Martin's head nodded vigorously. "Yes, ma'am. Tom said that you thought I might know your sister and that you wanted to ask me a few questions." His voice had a strong twang which made his "i"s sound like "a"s. It was a common accent in the area.

"Did Tom talk to you about who my sister was?" She glanced over at Tom in question and then looked back to Martin's face to study his reaction.

"I believe he said her name was Danielle. I'm not great with names, though, so it don't ring a bell."

Charlie pulled out her phone. She had looked through pictures of Dani the past couple of days in preparation for this moment. She'd settled on a selfie that Dani had sent her from work one day. Dani was wearing purple scrubs and a wide smile.

Charlie turned the phone around to show Martin. "This was her."

Martin took a minute studying the picture. He ran his hand back and forth over his jaw with his eyes darting between Charlie and the phone. "I see it now. She got all the curves, and you got the height, but y'all got the same nose and mouth. What tribe?"

Charlie took a deep breath, trying to push down the irritation. She wasn't interested in sharing her genealogy with this man, especially after his comment regarding body types.

She pushed the phone back toward him. "Did you know her? She was a nurse at the hospital in town. Most people called her Dani."

"Course I knew her!" He threw up his hands like he thought she and her questions were stupid.

"How did you know her?"

"Well, I think we first met when I was having problems with my gallbladder. She was my nurse and fixed me up right good. That's probably been about ten years now. After that, I reckon I saw her a couple a times a year in the hospital. She was always nice." He smiled, looking pleased with himself that he had remembered his history with Dani so well.

"Did you know that she had a child?"

"How could I forget?" He smiled and shook his head at her. "I saw her at the hospital one day. She wasn't in scrubs, so I asked why not. She said her baby was just born and she was there for that. I asked her about her man, and she just laughed. Said she didn't need no man to make a baby. We talked about her gettin' a donor. I told her I'd done that. Next time I was in, I asked to see a picture. She showed me, and that's when I knew."

Charlie thought she knew what was coming, but she wanted to hear him say it. "What was it you knew?"

"That I was the father, of course!" This time he looked at her like she was incapable of adding two and two. His eyebrows were scrunched, and he was looking at her out of the side of his eye. She spared a glance at Tom and noticed he looked like he could barely contain his amusement.

"That baby looks just like me. I told her it had to be mine, but she just wouldn't listen. We talked about it every time I saw her. I wanted visitation. That baby's my blood, and it's my right." Charlie noticed the color rising in his cheeks and on his neck as he was talking. She didn't want to upset him, so she didn't bother pointing out that sperm donations didn't work that way, and anyway, Rainna looked nothing like him.

Martin stood up from his seat on the bed. Charlie shoved her chair back with her feet, a loud screech echoing in the room as it scraped against the floor. He walked to the table beside his bed and opened the lone drawer. She watched as he shuffled through the contents, pulling out a Rubik's cube, some chewing gum, and a few other items.

She looked at Tom and tilted her head trying to see if he had any idea what was going on. Tom shook his head and went back to watching as Martin rifled through the small drawer.

"Found it!" Martin pulled a photo from the drawer. He walked back over to his seat at the end of the bed. "Here." He reached his arm toward Charlie to show her the photo. "Don't she look just like me?"

Charlie felt the hairs on the back of her neck stand up and her eyes went wide. Her heart sped up as she looked down at the photo in his hand.

CHAPTER 13

—

In the picture, Rainna was in the swing at the park. Dani was just visible in the image giving her a push. Rainna was wearing some toddler-sized red shoes that Charlie remembered had still fit her at the time Dani died. The picture must have been taken shortly before Dani's death. Whoever took the photo hadn't been close to them, but it was unmistakable that it was Dani and Rainna.

She lifted her eyes to Martin. His smile was like a proud papa's. She turned to Tom and tried to alert him that she was freaking out. Why did this man have a photo of Rainna and Dani? Had he been stalking them? Tom must have realized something was off. He left his perch by the wall and walked over to stand beside Martin. His mouth dropped into an "o" as he took in the picture.

"Where did you—"

"Martin, did you know that Dani was killed?" Charlie and Tom had started talking simultaneously, but she kept going when he paused. She knew what he was going to ask, and while it was valid, it wasn't what she needed to know.

Charlie initially thought this interview was going to be a waste of her time. But now, she felt a knot of fear in the pit of her stomach. If he was stalking Dani, it wouldn't be too great of a leap to think that Charlie could be sitting with the man who killed her sister.

"Of course, I knew she died." Martin leaned forward, placing his elbows on his knees. He looked Charlie directly in the eye and quickly raised his eyebrows. "I killed her."

Charlie felt the breath leave her lungs as she slumped back in the chair, and she heard the crash as the phone she was holding hit the tile.

Charlie reached down to grab her phone. A webbing of shattered glass covered its face, but Martin's words were running through her head, keeping her preoccupied. Her screen protector, while failing to do its job, had at least kept the glass together.

Charlie felt light-headed with a tightening in her chest.

"Just kidding! You should see the look on your face!" Martin's head flew back, and a loud cackle erupted. He slapped his knee as he laughed uncontrollably.

Charlie looked to Tom only to see her feelings reflected in his blank, slack expression. Tom composed himself first and schooled his features before placing a firm hand on Martin's shoulder. The touch calmed Martin, and the laughing died down in intensity, but he was still chuckling in a subdued way that was making him hiccup.

"Martin," Tom's voice was firm. "I know you didn't kill Charlie's sister, but that's not something to joke about. I'm going to walk Charlie out, and I'll come back to finish up our conversation."

Tom knows Martin didn't do it? Charlie was going to be evicted from the room after a confession that left her reeling.

She wanted to ask more. She needed to ask more. "Tom, could I—"

"Charlie, let's go."

"But Tom—"

"Charlie. Now."

The look on his face said he would not argue with her on this.

The moment the door slammed, Charlie turned to face Tom. "What just happened in there?" A nurse walked past, and the reality of their location hit her. Charlie lowered her voice to a whisper, "He said he killed her."

Tom avoided her gaze, glanced around him, and cleared his throat. "And then he said he was joking. Let me walk you out, and I'll explain."

"Tom, can I please just go talk to him a little more?" She hated that she sounded like she was begging, but she knew she wouldn't get the chance again.

"I can't let you, Charlie. Let's step outside."

The sound of Charlie's boots echoed in the hallway as they made their way back to the entrance. Tom held the door open for her, and they stepped into the crisp air. The wind whipped Charlie's loose hair around her, and she could feel the tangles forming.

Charlie glanced around ensuring they were alone. "Are you going to explain what just happened?" Her hands were clenched in fists and her nails were leaving half-moons across her palms.

Tom's hands were in his pockets, and he was shifting back and forth on his feet. He lifted his gaze and looked Charlie directly in her eyes. "I owe you an apology. I shouldn't have allowed this meeting."

"That's all I get?" Charlie's voice came out much louder

than Tom had spoken, and she clenched her teeth. "No. That man," Charlie gestured back toward the hospital room, "said he killed my sister. He had a photo of her and my niece. I expect a hell of a lot more than an apology. You're going to tell me exactly what's going on. Now."

"I can't explain what happened in there. I will say I didn't expect it. I'm sorry. Joking about Dani's death isn't funny."

"Damn right it's not funny. What the hell?" She crossed her arms and glared at him.

"Charlie, please. I'm just as surprised as you. But I can explain about his alibi. He didn't do it. I didn't know it for sure when you called. I actually just found out earlier." Tom reached out and squeezed her shoulder. She wanted to be furious at him, but her muscles relaxed. Charlie knew Tom wouldn't have done anything to hurt her on purpose. And she had pushed him to let her meet Martin.

"Tom, I know you didn't set this meeting up to play a trick on me. But that's what it feels like. I respect that you have duties to your client, and you can't share everything with me, but would you please explain to me why you let me come to meet him today? And how do you know he didn't do it? The photo of Rainna is disturbing. He has a motive, even if he's one hundred percent wrong about it."

Charlie watched as a middle-aged woman got out of her car. They waited until the woman made her way past them and into the building.

Tom scratched his jaw. "I told you I'm not convinced that Darius did it. I'm glad you're interested in making sure that everything is right with this. You wanted to meet Martin, and I thought if you started looking into things, doing the legwork, it would spur your curiosity. Maybe you'd have to keep going. I was almost positive I could prove that Martin didn't do it when you asked, and I thought he might enjoy the company. He doesn't get many visitors."

Charlie pressed her lips together. "So, this was all a giant waste of my time?"

Tom tugged at his collar. "I don't think so. I think you should be looking into Dani's death. There's a reason why something doesn't seem right to you. It's your life. You should be sure of what happened to your own sister.

"Don't take this the wrong way, but you're capable of more, Charlie. You work at home and you take care of Rainna. It's all you've done since Dani died. You're a shadow of who you could be. I thought maybe looking into this would bring back some of that fire that Winnie always talked about from when you were young."

Charlie used the toe of her boot to push some pebbles across the ground and swallowed past the lump forming in her throat. *Am I really a shadow?* "What about the photo? Did you know about that?"

"I swear I've never seen that photo before." Tom held up his hands. "I don't know where Martin got it—if he took it or someone else did. I agree with you that it's disturbing. If he wasn't already on a strict security protocol, I would talk to them about ramping it up." Tom looked apologetic.

"I'm reserving the right to bring up the issue about the photo later. Especially if I ever hear that he's no longer institutionalized." She stopped for a moment to allow a man to exit the facility and get to his car.

"What was with the confession? And the laughing?" Charlie asked.

"Charlie, I really don't know. I assume it's something to do with his condition, but he does have an odd sense of humor. Maybe it was just that. What I can tell you is that he didn't do it. After I texted you the other day, I got the final set of records I'd requested. He was in a facility when Dani died. The logs show that he was checked on every three hours. I've lined up their log with the timing of Dani's death. It's not possible."

Charlie kept moving a pebble with her toe while she tried to gather her thoughts. She pulled the sweater tighter around her middle as the wind punished her, "I do trust you, Tom," she looked up at him, "but I would really like to see a copy of those records."

"I understand. But they're medical records, so let me see what I can do to redact information and get any necessary permissions." Tom glanced at the screen on his phone, reminding Charlie that she now had to get hers replaced. "Look, Charlie, I'm sorry. This didn't go like I thought. But I've got to get back in there and take care of some things before I head to my next appointment."

"Alright. Bye, Tom." Charlie heard Tom say goodbye as he made his way inside, and she went to her Jeep.

She turned the key in the ignition and noticed her hands were shaking. She couldn't keep all this to herself. She couldn't call Winnie, even if Tom knew everything. This would be something Tom wouldn't tell Winnie. He wouldn't want her to know he didn't trust the police's investigation and he was encouraging Charlie to investigate on her own.

She pulled her phone out of her back pocket, groaning as she looked at the broken screen.

Charlie: You will not believe the day I had.

Three dots appeared immediately.

Malachi: Tell me.

Charlie: I met the guy who thought he was the sperm donor.

Malachi: Will you call me?

Charlie: Give me 20 minutes. I need to drive home first.

Malachi: I'll be waiting.

She got home fifteen minutes later. She let Buck out, kicked off her boots, and paced downstairs a couple of times before pulling out her phone. She pulled up Malachi's number on the cracked screen and pressed the phone icon as she sat on the floor, leaning back against the couch.

"Are you okay?" Malachi sounded worried.

"I… I don't know," she said quietly, rubbing her legs to ease some of the tension in her muscles. "Today was definitely one for the books."

"Please tell me you didn't go meet this guy all by yourself. What were you thinking?"

"Wait," she shook her head, "I thought you liked that I was looking into this."

"I don't want you doing something stupid that could get you hurt. Someone killed your sister and they're still out there. Others may not believe that, but I do. They wouldn't be too excited to know you're trying to find them."

"I appreciate your concern. But I'm a big girl. And I wasn't by myself. I was with a friend."

Charlie let out the breath she was holding and let her head fall back. "Just let me tell you about it, okay?" Heat spread up the back of her neck at his concern. She felt a little like a child caught climbing too high at the playground.

"Okay," he said slowly. "You're right and I'm listening." She could still hear his concern, but his agitation had disappeared, and she knew she would have his full attention.

Charlie told Malachi the short version of how she found out about Martin from Winnie. How she had asked the guy's lawyer if she could meet him. Then, she walked him through her morning. She left out details that would identify Martin, but otherwise, she told him as much as she could.

He never interrupted her but would make small "hmm" or "huh" sounds to let her know he was following.

When she told him Martin said he killed Dani, she heard a sharp intake of breath, but he still didn't interrupt. She finished by telling him that he said he was joking, and Tom accounted for Martin's whereabouts for the night Dani died. There were time logs to prove it. She let out a shaky breath and let silence fill the line.

After several seconds, Malachi's voice came through. "You need to inform the police about the photo. I don't care if this guy couldn't have done it, he could be a danger to you and Rainna, and you need to make sure others are aware."

"I'm thinking about it. The photo has me freaked out, but at least I know that he's not the one who killed Dani. It doesn't seem like he's looking for Rainna. I don't know, it's all so strange. I'm pretty sure Tom would understand if I talked to the cops about it. It's not like the guy's gonna get arrested for it, just maybe watched more closely. Seeing the photo might have been even creepier than when he said he killed Dani. It made me scared for Rainna." Charlie's stomach churned thinking about the photo and she wrapped her arm around her middle.

"I don't think you have anything to worry about with Rainna as long as this guy's not in the picture."

"Yeah." Charlie went silent again, replaying everything from the morning. She hadn't really thought Martin killed

Dani, but now she didn't know what step to take next. The opportunity to talk to Martin had fallen in her lap. It was easy to meet him without feeling like she was really pursuing this case. Did she want to go full speed ahead with investigating? Her only other lead was Dani's ex, Liam Sullivan. He was a doctor in a small town. In other words, he was a golden boy. No one would believe anything bad of him. She would need solid proof, and finding that seemed unlikely three years after the fact.

"I think I have to let this go. It's taking over my thoughts. I don't know where to go next. I don't think Darius did it, but I honestly don't know who could have. I don't think there were any other suspects. Maybe you can hire an investigator." She dragged her hand across her face. "I don't know what I'm doing. I was just trying to answer lingering questions; now I've only created more." She crossed her arms and brought her right hand to her mouth, chewing on her thumbnail and trying to quell the jittery feeling in her hands and feet.

"Charlie, stop." Malachi's voice was firm. "No one ever asked you to do this. Not Darius. Not me. We only asked you to consider he might not have done it. You started down this road. If you want to keep going, you need to do that for yourself."

"You're right." Her sigh filled the line. "I just feel all this pressure right now. Not from you. It's internal. It's like I need to figure this out for me and for Rainna. Like I would not only be letting Dani down but letting myself down because I had a question that I couldn't find the answer to. But how do I even start?"

"Well, how do people do it on TV? Don't they start by retracing the victim's steps from the last couple of days before the crime? Maybe you retrace Dani's steps," Malachi said.

The tone made her think he was joking, but his comment got to her. She had talked to Dani on the phone several hours before she died, but what else had Dani done?

"Look, Charlie. If you don't find the answer you're looking for, no one will ever think less of you. Darius and I will keep looking for ways to fight this, with or without you. It just makes me feel good to have someone willing to consider a different possible ending to this story."

Silence filled the line and Charlie took a few calming breaths. A far away voice on Malachi's end reached her ears, "Mr. Thomas, your next appointment has been here for fifteen minutes."

"Malachi, I'm so sorry! I didn't mean to make you late. Go. Thanks for letting me unload on you. I really appreciate it."

"No problem. Bye, Charlie. I hope we can talk again soon."

Charlie hung up and lay down on the rug in front of the couch. Buck came over and started licking her face. "What do we do now, buddy? What do we do now?"

CHAPTER 14

Charlie pulled a leaf apart while she sat cross-legged on the hard ground. She'd been sitting there for a while and the cold had seeped through her pants, making her legs stiff.

"What do I do, Dan?" she asked, looking at the simple granite headstone. Charlie had driven to the cemetery after dropping Rainna off at school. She didn't visit often. She knew Dani wasn't there, but Charlie had discovered the calming effect of talking through her issues and problems out loud after her mother had died. Charlie could be found in front of one of their gravestones whenever she was working through a dilemma.

"I don't know how to do this. I make food, and I write about it. I don't know anything about investigating a murder. I don't know how." She plucked a few blades of grass and listened to the wind.

"I wish I could get rid of this feeling—the one that's telling me something isn't right. But it won't go away. And I know going to talk to Martin yesterday was probably stupid, but it felt right in the moment. To be doing something. Moving forward. Talking to a suspect instead of just reading. Even if I did an epically bad job of it. I wish Ethan could consider the possibility that they got it wrong. I wish it didn't have to be me." A bouquet of fresh daisies was in the vase attached to the headstone and Charlie grabbed one. They were always here, the daisies. Dani had loved tulips, but they were hard to come by at this time of the year, and Charlie thought Dani would appreciate whoever had left them.

A petal came off in her hand and she thought of the children's game, He loves me, He loves me not.

"Okay, Dan. Let's leave it to chance. I drop it, or I keep looking." Pulling the petals off the daisy one by one, she whispered, "I drop it" and "I keep looking." She got to the end and took a deep breath as she grabbed the last petal, "I keep looking."

"I guess I've got to figure this out." She stood up and stretched, her bones popping. She kissed her fingers and touched the headstone. "Miss you, Dan."

Malachi's comment about retracing Dani's steps was stuck in Charlie's head. When she got home, she made a list of everything she could remember from her last phone conversations with Dani.

- *Date with Darius*
- *Rough shift at work—patient died, something happened with Liam*
- *Dad stopped by to play with Rainna*
- *Dani had a swing set built in the backyard for Rainna*
- *Rainna moved to a new class in school*
- *Dani volunteered at church blood drive*

Charlie was sure there were other things, but those were the details she remembered. Charlie also had Dani's banking records, and she had pulled everything from the last several months of Dani's life. If anything was to be found, though, Charlie wasn't the one to find it. She saw payments for bills, deposits from work, purchases from the grocery store, coffee shop, and some local cafes. Boring stuff.

The news articles regarding Dani's death and the trial were more awkward for Charlie to go through. Keeping all the articles about her sister's death felt macabre, but throwing them away hadn't felt like an option either. The first article started out simple enough with a mere statement of facts and the heading, "Police Investigate Local Nurse's Death as Possible Homicide." However, that was quickly followed by "Suspect in Custody for Murder of Local Nurse" and "Single Mother Murdered by Boyfriend." The articles didn't give many details on the investigation. No other suspects or persons of interest were named.

She knew she needed to talk to one person—Dani's ex-boyfriend and boss, Liam Sullivan. Ethan said Liam's alibi was solid, but she still wanted to verify. She also felt like she should talk to some of Dani's coworkers and friends. Maybe they would give her a better idea of what had been going on with Dani in those last days. They saw her more than anyone else. Could Dani have been arguing with Darius or maybe Liam? It was a shame that her father was no longer around. He may have known something before he died that could be helpful in finding out what really happened.

To try and figure this out, she needed to do more than read transcripts and reports. Those things gave her a framework of information, but she didn't think they would hold the answers. It should have been the least of her worries, but she hated the idea of people thinking she didn't trust the police investigation. That wasn't something the people around here would like.

If Ethan gave her the police report, it would help her know who had been interviewed. Ethan wanted to talk to her about a relationship, and she wanted to speak to him about the report. He hadn't gotten back to her about it since she brought it up at the ice cream shop. Unfortunately, he had something she wanted, and she knew the best hand she could play in the game was herself.

Time to bite the bullet.

> **Charlie:** Hey, could we talk about the report? I'll buy you dinner.
>
> **Ethan:** I would love to take you out to dinner! Saturday at 7, we'll go to Frankie's.
>
> **Charlie:** I'll see if I can find a sitter.
>
> **Ethan:** Winnie's probably out. She told me West is having a big sleepover for his birthday that night.
>
> **Charlie:** I'll check with Betti

Asking Betti for help would mean the whole town would know that Charlie and Ethan were dating by close of business, but that was a risk she was willing to take. She was sick of this waffling feeling, never knowing if she thought Darius did it. And now, thanks to Martin, she was also worried about Rainna.

> **Charlie:** Hey, Betti! Could you watch Rainna for me on Saturday night?
>
> **Betti:** What are you doing that would make you need a sitter? ;)
>
> **Charlie:** Ethan and I are going to Frankie's.
>
> **Betti:** Ooooo, it's about time you wised up! Sure, I would love to!!! Can she stay the night?

Charlie: I'm fine picking her up when we're done, but if it would be easier for you, she can stay the night.

Charlie: I'll watch your kids sometime soon if you want to take a day for yourself.

Betti: Yes!!!!! I'll let you know when!

Betti's kids were a little much for Charlie, but from what she'd heard, Betti and her husband were still separated. Winnie said a much younger woman was in the picture.

The rest of the day went by in a blur, with Charlie lining up a podcast appearance and a special guest spot on a popular YouTube Channel for the next week. She was also dealing with trolls on her website. On Saturday night, Charlie was pulling on her black skinny jeans when a pounding came from the front door.

"Rain, I think Betti's here. Could you grab your bag and get the door?"

"Yep! Be right there!" The sound of a zipper was followed by tiny feet pounding down the stairs.

Charlie was touching up her mascara when she heard boots on the floor too heavy to belong to Betti. Charlie's heart rate picked up, and her stomach clenched. Martin's picture of Dani and Rainna flashed through her head as she raced down the stairs, catching herself right before she tripped over Buck at the bottom.

"Well, don't you look excited to see me." Ethan gave her a self-assured smile and winked. "I'm pretty happy to see you, too. But you probably need shoes for our date."

Charlie glanced down at her bare feet and tank top. The fear she'd felt only a moment before was quickly replaced with heat on her cheeks.

"You're early." Charlie couldn't think of anything better

to say than to state the obvious.

"Cops are always early. I'm glad, too, because I got to see this little princess." He ruffled Rainna's hair, and she looked at him with bright eyes as she hugged his legs.

"So, do you want to tell her, or should I?" Ethan looked at Rainna with a smirk. Charlie felt a prickle of apprehension.

"Me! Me! Guess what, Auntie? I asked Ethan and he's going to take me to the daddy/daughter Christmas dance next week! Isn't that awesome?"

"Wow. That's… that's, um, that's really great, sweets." *Daddy/daughter dance?* "Um, what day is that, again?" Charlie couldn't decide if she was more upset that Rainna hadn't told her about the dance, that she asked Ethan without her permission, or that Ethan said yes without talking to her.

"Next Thursday!" Rainna squealed while dancing around them.

"What's next Thursday?" Charlie jumped at Betti's voice coming from the open front door. Buck let out a sharp bark too late to alert her to the new visitor.

"Ethan's taking me to the daddy/daughter dance, Betti!" Rainna squeaked.

"Well, well, well. Ain't that sweet." Betti waggled her eyebrows at Charlie. "Alright, kiddo, let's head out. Your aunt's got herself a hot date, and we've got some pizza to pick up."

Charlie snagged Rainna around the waist as she started to run out the door. She picked her up and flipped her over to blow a raspberry on her tummy, making Rainna dissolve into a fit of giggles. "Love you, sweets. Be good," Charlie whispered in her hair as she hugged and kissed Rainna.

Charlie was watching Rainna head out when Ethan cleared his throat. She looked up at him, and he was looking at her bare feet. "Oh, be right back."

They rode in Ethan's car to a family-style Italian restaurant about thirty minutes away. Most of the ride was spent in awkward small talk about jobs and things around the town.

The moments of silence when the conversation lulled gave Charlie a chance to think. Rainna usually told her about the events at school, but she hadn't heard anything about the dance. Rainna had been acting quiet lately. Was the dance why Rainna had been a little off? Was she sad about not having someone to go to the dance with her? Was she missing her grandpa? Was she keeping anything else from Charlie?

Charlie and her father's relationship had been rocky and volatile since her mother had died. His move to try to get custody of Rainna rather than letting Charlie raise her hadn't improved the tension. But he had loved Rainna fiercely and had done what he could to be a positive male role model in her life. Rainna had already been through so much loss, and she wasn't even five yet.

At the restaurant, Ethan tried to order food for them, but Charlie knew exactly what she liked when it came to Frankie's, and she wasn't having anyone ruin her experience. Frankie's had an impressive menu, but their spaghetti and meatballs was the best dish. It was rich, the sauce was perfect, and it reminded her of childhood.

When the waiter had taken their order, Charlie swallowed her pride. "Thank you for agreeing to take Rainna to the dance. That was kind of you." She wanted to be mad at Ethan about the situation, but the drive over made her realize that it was more important for Rainna to have this moment. To be able to go to the dance and not feel different from the other kids.

"It's no problem. I like being around Rainna. I'm glad I get to do this for her. And for you."

Charlie put her chin in her palm and smiled. "Well, if you like doing things for me, you could always let me have a copy of your file." Charlie didn't want to wait until the end of the night to ask; especially not when she had a sneaking suspicion that she wouldn't be in the best mood by the time the night was over.

"Charlie, I don't understand why you think it would do you any good. You know the outcome. Why do the steps matter? It's not going to change anything."

"If it's not going to change anything, that's all the more reason to let me see it. Ethan, you know how I am. I'm pretty sure you've called me a dog with a bone before. I've decided that seeing it will make me feel better. I asked you like I did because I don't want to cause a big stir. But it's a closed case, so I can legally request a copy and you shouldn't be able to deny my request." She took a drink of her water, wiping the condensation from the glass on the cloth napkin in her lap. They were seated across from each other at a two-top near the back of the restaurant, which was quiet other than the clinking of silverware on plates and soft murmuring.

Ethan leaned toward her on his elbows. "Hey, we just got here. This is nothing to get worked up over. I went ahead and pulled it out the other day after you asked about it. I might need to redact a few things. I understand that you can legally have a copy. I'm not trying to be a jerk. I just want you to think about why you're wasting your time this way."

Charlie dove into the bread basket to keep herself from arguing. She had broached the topic she wanted to discuss, and she felt a bubble of triumph that he'd already pulled the file. But she was all too aware that he could take his sweet time handing over what she wanted.

Ethan spent the time waiting for their dinner telling Charlie about the middle school baseball team he helped coach. He had encouraged her to come and watch several times during the season, but she didn't like baseball. "You should really get more involved around here. I know you don't like sports all that much, but maybe you could help out with the track team or mentor some of the kids on the school newspaper," Ethan said.

Charlie picked at the bread on her plate. "I don't really like kids all that much. And I don't see how I could help them any more than their teachers already do."

"Char, don't be like that. You avoiding everyone and not getting involved is exactly why people say what they do."

Charlie set the bread on her plate and sat up in her chair. "What exactly do people say about me?"

"Don't use that tone. You know that you haven't even tried to get into the swing of things since you moved back."

The waiter walked up with a tray laden with food, and they dropped the conversation for a moment. Twirling her spaghetti around on her fork, Charlie tried to decide whether she really wanted to know what people were saying about her. She was two-thirds through her plate when Ethan cleared his throat.

"Charlie, I know you've spent the last few years focused on Rainna. But it's time you think about what you want in your life. You know I've had a thing for you for forever. I don't care that you left or what you did while you were gone. We're not getting any younger. Are you going to give us a chance? I think it would be good for you, and if tonight's any indication, it would be good for Rainna. That girl needs a man in her life. I still can't believe Dani thought a sperm donor was a good idea. Every kid needs a father."

Anger flared in her chest at the comment about Dani. Charlie placed her fork on the edge of her plate. She ran a hand over her face and tucked her hair behind her ear. Rainna probably did need another parent, but that didn't mean Charlie would get married again. She'd made enough sacrifices by moving back to her hometown to raise Rainna around people who knew and loved her. Charlie couldn't tie herself to another person for the sake of giving Rainna a father figure. "Ethan, I feel like we keep having the same conversation."

"—but you wouldn't be here if you didn't feel something between us."

"Ethan, please let me finish. I don't deny that we have a history. But it ended, and you had a part in that."

"We were kids back then. I'm not the one who started all that and I can't believe you're still holding that against me." His whisper was harsh.

Charlie refolded the napkin in her lap, smoothing the edges. This was one of her favorite meals, but the company was making it less appetizing than usual. She was about to ask Ethan if they could head out when she heard a smooth male voice, "Ethan! You didn't tell me you had a date tonight. Who's the lucky lady?"

CHAPTER 15

———

Charlie turned to see who had walked up behind her. Dr. Liam Sullivan was reaching out to shake Ethan's hand. He glanced toward her, and his posture stiffened. She recognized his brown side-parted hair and straight nose from photos Dani had shown Charlie from when she dated him.

"Liam, I believe you know Charlie." Ethan smiled and stood to talk to Liam.

"No," Charlie said. "We've never actually met." Charlie rose from her chair and stuck her hand out. Liam had moved to town after Charlie had left for college. Although her sister had dated Liam on and off for a while, his schedule never allowed them to meet when she was in town visiting. Liam was staring at Charlie, still shaking her hand long after he should have let go. A lovely, petite blonde woman touched his elbow, drawing Charlie's attention.

"I'm Liam's wife, Savanna." Charlie gave a smile worthy of a pageant contestant when she turned to shake Savanna's hand.

"Nice to meet you, Savanna." The petite woman seemed to size Charlie up but quickly shifted her attention back to the men like Charlie was irrelevant. Charlie noticed a rock on Savanna's hand that would put anything else in a thirty-mile radius to shame. "Your ring is lovely. Have you been married long?"

Savanna wiggled her fingers and glanced adoringly at the ring on her finger and then at her husband. "Three years next month."

"It looks like the waiter's got our table ready, better not keep him waiting. Charlie, nice meeting you. Enjoy your evening. Ethan, I'll see you at the gym in the morning." As Charlie, Ethan, and Savanna said their goodbyes, Liam placed his hand on his wife's back and pushed her toward their table.

Three years next month? Dani had been dating Liam on and off until a few months before she died, when she finally broke it off and started dating Darius. Could he have been dating Savanna and Dani at the same time?

And had he always been so chummy with Ethan? They worked out together? It could have been nothing, but it felt suspect.

Charlie told Ethan she was full and asked to head out. As he drove back, his talk of working out and watching football sounded like buzzing in her ears. When he dropped her off, he tried to hold her hand as he walked her to the door, but she shook him off.

"Ethan," she said as he was walking to his car from her door.

"Yeah?" he asked.

"I really hope you'll let me have that file."

He turned and kept walking, but she thought she heard him say under his breath, "I really hoped you'd say something different."

As she went to sleep that night, Charlie was still trying to figure out how to find out more about the alibi of Dr. Liam

Sullivan. Long after Charlie's date with Ethan was over, she kept thinking about how Liam had married very quickly after ending things with her sister.

* * *

Minimizing the seven tabs she had open on her laptop, she felt a touch of embarrassment. She had spent the last day looking up everything she could find on Dr. Liam Sullivan and his wife, Savanna. Charlie wanted to see if she could find out if they had been together while Liam had something with Dani. Liam didn't appear to have any social media profiles, but his wife did. And it definitely looked like they were together at the same time.

Charlie couldn't know for sure, but it seemed unlikely that Dani knew about Savanna. Liam and Dani's relationship mostly took place before Rainna. Dani had told Charlie that Liam wasn't comfortable with how she chose to have Rainna, but they had still dated a few times after Rainna arrived.

A chime alerted Charlie to a text, and it synced to her computer screen before she had a chance to grab her phone.

> **Malachi:** Hey, please don't feel any pressure to say yes, but I have a meeting in Tulsa later this week I was wondering if I could swing by and see you on my drive back. I got a copy of the arson expert's full report from the defense attorney since you mentioned being interested in it.

Charlie froze. Was she ready to meet Malachi in person? She had enjoyed their talks and messages, but she'd never considered anything further.

Malachi: It's okay if you can't.

Charlie hesitated briefly and then went with her gut.

Charlie: That sounds great! Let me know when you're leaving Tulsa.

Charlie felt the nerves in her stomach at the thought of meeting Malachi in person. Since they had been communicating, she had tried not to dwell too much on who Malachi was in relation to her, even though their odd connection was how they met. Instead, she thought of him as her Dallas friend. The one she could talk to about town stuff that she wasn't comfortable sharing with her friends here, like the woman who told her son not to play with Rainna at school because "bad things happened to Allen girls."

The following morning was the day the Family and Consumer Science teacher had set up for Charlie to talk to students and teach a cooking class. She had arranged this before Ethan had called her out on not integrating herself in the town, but she hadn't told him about it because there was no point. He wanted her to volunteer on a regular basis at the school, but that wasn't for her. After checking in with the school's receptionist, she made her way to the class. She was pleased to see that everything was set up and ready exactly the way she requested.

When the bell rang, about twenty teenagers filed in and made their way to their workstations. The teacher briefly introduced Charlie and then turned the class over to her.

"Good morning, everyone. I'm Charlie Allen. I've been a food blogger for several years now and Mrs. Reisner asked me to talk to you about creating recipes. I can also answer questions you may have about my job. While we talk, I'm going to walk you through my basic scone recipe. You have several options on the workstations for the flavors you would like to use in your own scones, so each of you will get to choose."

She talked them through the steps to combine the dry ingredients and then brought them cold butter when it was time to cut it into the flour. Mrs. Reisner motioned that she was going to step out for a moment but for Charlie to keep going. As Charlie walked around the class helping students, she told them about the small batches she would make when working on a recipe, adjusting one ingredient at a time so she could understand the impact that ingredient had on the whole. The students were busy cutting the butter into their dry ingredients when she opened the floor for questions.

A young man with black hair and baggy clothes raised his hand. "Is it true you lit your apartment on fire cooking?"

The heads of the other students snapped to Charlie and she let out a small laugh. "Yes, sort of. Well… I used too much alcohol in a dessert fondue, and it caused a fire in my apartment. Luckily the fire didn't reach anything and we were able to use the fire extinguisher to put it out quickly."

"Didn't your sister die in a fire?" he asked. He turned to the girl at the workstation with him and said, "Seems a little fishy to me."

A flare of irritation hit Charlie and she had to remind herself that she was talking to a teenager. "Yes. My sister died in a fire. And not that it's in any way relevant to this class, but I was in a different state when it happened."

Before she finished, the rest of the students in the room started chatting amongst themselves. A few were brave enough to make themselves heard.

"I heard you don't believe the guy who's locked up actually did it. Is that true?"

"Hush, Tawny. Of course the guy did it. He's going to rot in prison. My dad says this lady just has a stick up her ass. She thinks she knows better than the police, the judge, and the jury."

"I bet it was a serial killer. You always hear about those strangers who break in—"

"Guy who's in prison definitely did it. He was a drug dealer."

"I live down the road from where she lived. Guys were always over there. Ma said no one was ever gonna buy that cow 'cause she was givin' away the milk for free. Maybe there was another lover. Some sorta twisty love triangle."

"It's always the boyfriend or the husband."

"Or a family member. Stranger killings aren't really a thing."

Charlie's head had been moving back and forth watching the different speakers as they each put forth their theories. Her scones, along with the reason for being there, were forgotten.

"Class!" Mrs. Reisner yelled as she walked back into the room. "That's enough. You are being incredibly disrespectful to our guest. I want you all to apologize to Ms. Allen right now."

"That's okay. No apology necessary. You all are curious, and you have opinions. I get that." Charlie shook her head trying to remember what she had been doing before the class went haywire. "Who knows," she said looking directly at the boy who freely gave his dad's opinion of her, "maybe I do have a stick up my ass." Mrs. Reisner gasped and pulled the boy to the side.

A small part of her was embarrassed that she hadn't gotten the class back under control herself. But she'd been too caught up in what they were saying. Most people didn't talk about their opinions of the case in front of her, so it was interesting to hear their theories.

The rest of the class was uneventful as she finished her instructions. Questions focused on influencer status on social media and several girls wanting to know how to make themselves more marketable.

When the bell rang, Charlie was glad to see the students go. They filed out with half-hearted thank yous as Charlie grabbed a rag to help the teacher clean up.

"I'm really sorry for that. I had no idea something like that would happen," Mrs. Reisner said as Charlie handed her back the rag after wiping down the workstations.

"It's fine," Charlie waved her hand. She knew teenagers were unpredictable and didn't blame the teacher. As uncomfortable as it had been to finish the class after hearing unflattering opinions of herself and her sister, she at least appreciated how unfiltered young people could be. Older people said it behind her back. At least these kids said it to her face.

It was lunch break as Charlie was leaving school. The halls were empty, except for a few stragglers. She glanced into the classrooms as she went by, remembering moments from her high school days in the building she was walking through.

As she passed the second to last door on the left before the exit, she saw a familiar face at the front of the room.

"Hey, Zack," Charlie said with a quick knock on the open door. The teacher behind the desk stood up and made his way over to her spot by the door. Zack O'Connor was a year older than Charlie and they had gone to school together. He had messy brown hair and his plaid shirt was tucked into his khakis. He was a history teacher and coach at the high school.

"Charlie Allen. What are you doing here?" he asked.

"Mrs. Reisner asked me to teach a class to the FCS students. I just finished up."

"Oh yeah?" He raised his eyebrows. "How'd it go?"

"Let's just say that I won't be getting my teaching certificate any day soon," she said with a wry smile, remembering how completely out of control she had let the class get.

They talked for a few minutes catching up. His wife had also gone to school with them and she had recently given birth to their third child. A buzzing sound started and Charlie opened her purse to see if it was her phone.

"It's me," Zack said, pulling his phone out of his pocket. "Crap."

"Everything okay?" Charlie asked as Zack ran his hand over his head.

"There's a wreck out by the mountain. Someone took the turn too quick and went over the railing."

"Oh wow. I hope they're okay," Charlie said. Unfortunately, too many people had made the same mistake and some of them hadn't lived to tell the tale.

"Yeah. I always feel like I should be helping. Even when I'm here and I'm not on call," Zack said, rubbing his hands together.

"Oh yeah, I forgot. You're a volunteer with the fire department."

"Eight years now." He smiled as he put his hands in his pockets. He had always been one of those people who was active in a lot of different things—football, honor society, academic team, and the church youth group. It made sense to Charlie that he would spend his time volunteering with the fire department.

"Eight years, wow. That's wonderful," Charlie said, as she thought about spending that many years helping others in life-threatening situations for no other reason than wanting to be helpful. "Wait. Did you... were you there that night?" she asked him. Could he have been one of the first people on the scene when Dani died?

"What night?" he asked.

"The night Dani died?"

Zack's gaze dropped to his feet as he shifted back and forth. He cleared his throat. "Yeah. I was there."

Charlie's heart rate picked up. "You were?"

He nodded, his eyes still on his shoes. "We had just finished up another call when dispatch sent us to Dani's house."

"Do you... Could I... Um..." She stopped and shook her head. "Could I ask you some questions about that night?" He hadn't been one of the witnesses at the trial, so Charlie hadn't realized Zack had been there. Maybe he could walk her through what he had seen.

He shook his head, "I'm sorry, Charlie. But no."

"What?" Charlie asked, confused by his answer. Her sister was dead and he had been there on the scene. Why wouldn't he talk to her about it? "It'll just be a few minutes. I promise. Or if now's a bad time, I could swing by and talk to you about it later."

"Charlie, I'm sorry about Dani, but I don't want to talk about that night."

"I don't understand. Why?"

"It was one of the worst in my career. It's always hard to see people die. But when it's someone you've known your whole life... I can't explain it." He finally lifted his eyes to hers. "And Dani, well, she was special. I always admired her. How beautiful she was, and the way she cared for people." She could hear the strain in his voice like he was holding back tears. "I know you think you deserve to know things, but you don't get to make me relive it. I'd heard you were asking for information on the trial and the investigation. I'd hoped it wasn't true. I trust the investigation that took place and I'm not going to be a part of whatever you're up to. So no, you can't ask me questions about that night."

"But—" she started, but he shook his head and she knew he wouldn't change his mind. Resolve was etched into his features and she no longer felt welcome at his door.

"I... Okay," she said. The bell rang and voices and footsteps filled the halls once more.

"I'm going to head out. Congratulations on the baby." Charlie walked to the exit of the school feeling like she had the time she fell off a four-wheeler and into a pile of mud—embarrassed and a little bruised.

CHAPTER 16

—

Charlie was holding her phone in one hand and chewing on her thumbnail with the other.

Malachi: Leaving my meeting now. I'll be there in a couple of hours. Where do you want me to meet you?

The events of the day before at the school still had Charlie rattled. The thought of meeting Malachi now made her stomach churn. It wasn't anything to do with him. His texts and their conversations had been a light for her the last few weeks, but everything seemed to be snowballing.

Charlie gave Malachi her address, cranked up Nirvana's *Nevermind* album and threw herself into cooking to quiet her mind. Rainna was at school, so Charlie didn't have to worry about the awkward conversation of who Malachi was and why he was coming over to the house.

As she was blowing on a spoon to cool what she was tasting, Buck's nails clicked on the hardwood followed by a bark and the doorbell. A glance at her watch let her know she had lost track of time.

Tugging the hem of her shirt and running a hand over her head to smooth the flyaways, Charlie jerked the door open and looked up. She'd never stood next to Malachi, so she was surprised when he took up the entire door frame. His beard was shorter than she remembered from when she saw him at the trial. He was holding a paper bag and shuffling his feet. When she looked into his eyes, he looked unsure but gave her a slight smirk. Seeing that he was nervous broke the tension for Charlie, and she smiled.

"Um," Malachi started to talk and move toward Charlie like he was going for a hug when he stopped himself. Charlie found his uncertainty endearing and took pity on him by reaching forward for a quick hug.

Pulling back, she looked into his eyes. "It's good to see you."

"It's good to see you, too." He cleared his throat. "Is this weird?"

Charlie shrugged. "Of course, it's weird." She shook her head at him. "How could it not be? But just because it's weird doesn't mean it's bad." Charlie's nerves from the morning were gone, and she just wanted to make him feel less awkward.

Malachi followed her into the house and looked down at the bag in his hands. "I brought you something. Nothing big, but I thought you might enjoy it. But just a warning, you have to share. I waited in line for this, and now I've got to know if it was worth it."

Charlie eyed the bag in Malachi's hands and saw the tiny writing on the front. It was from a new bakery in Tulsa that she'd been dying to try. She snatched the bag out of his hands. She opened it, breathing in the chocolate and butter and brown sugar that immediately hit her nostrils. "You brought me Neon's?" Malachi nodded. "We've only known each other a short time, and you already get that the way to my heart is through my stomach. It feels good to be understood." She looked up and gave him a rare smile.

Malachi shrugged his shoulders like it was nothing. Charlie broke a piece off a cookie. She popped half in her mouth and handed the other half to Malachi.

"Mmmm... so good." She savored the chocolate as she chewed. "Okay, I made you lunch. Let's eat that first, and then we can finish off this dessert."

"You made me lunch?" He reached up and pulled at his collar. They were both still standing like they weren't sure what to do.

"Yeah. Nothing fancy, butternut squash soup and savory scones. I had to teach a class on scones yesterday, so I was craving these." Charlie moved to grab a couple of bowls. "Does that work?"

"Sounds great," he cleared his throat. "Nobody ever makes me food except for my mom. I'm an awful cook, so I'll take any homemade food I can get." Malachi smiled, and Charlie was glad she'd gone to the effort. Cooking for people who didn't appreciate it always bothered Charlie, but there wasn't much that she enjoyed more than cooking for people who did.

They ate their lunch and talked about Malachi's meeting and Charlie's Christmas preparations. Charlie found Malachi easy to talk to, and their conversation found a steady rhythm. After the meal, Charlie decided to tackle the elephant in the room. "How is Darius doing?"

"I think he's okay. He's been spending a lot of time in the library, trying to help some of the other guys with their appeals. He feels bad that so many of the guys in there can't afford a lawyer, and since their trials are over, the ones they had dropped them. He's not an expert, but he understands this stuff better than a lot of the other guys. It's good for him to have something to focus on."

Charlie didn't know how to respond. When the silence had stretched, she said, "I haven't made it much further looking into everything. There's just so much I don't know. But I took your advice and tried to find out as much as I could about what Dani did in the days before she died. I ran into a guy yesterday who was one of the first responders. I hadn't realized he'd been there that night, but when I asked him about it, he shut me down."

"Why?"

"He said it was one of his worst nights. He didn't want to relive it. And he thought I was wasting my time. It's fine. It makes sense why he wouldn't want to talk to me." She gathered the dishes and avoided looking at Malachi. "Do you want to see my notes?" He nodded. Charlie went to get her computer and notebooks and took them into the dining room at the front of the house.

She sat at the table with Malachi beside her, both looking at the computer and notes between them on the table. He placed a hand on her shoulder and squeezed as she told him that she didn't know where to go next without more information.

A sharp bark from Buck at the front door pulled Charlie's attention from her lists. Three loud knocks followed.

Charlie made her way to the door, pulling it open to see Ethan at the door holding a large manilla folder. She couldn't miss the scowl on his face or that he was looking behind her into the house. The curtains in the dining room were open, and he could have seen her with Malachi through the window on his way to the front door.

"Ethan, what brings you by?" She glanced at the package in his hands, hoping it was what she wanted. She tried to will him not to turn around and take it with him.

"Is that what this is all about?" He pointed into the house and then lifted the package in his hands.

When Charlie didn't respond, Ethan looked at her with contempt. "I don't even know who you are anymore. Bringing the brother of your sister's murderer into the house where your niece lives. Is he why you wanted this?" He held up the folder.

He headed down the front porch steps and then turned back to Charlie. "You know what? I do think you need to file an official request, after all. You'll need to come by the station and fill out the paperwork with Anita. I think it takes about ten business days to review the requests. No favors."

Charlie followed him down the steps, "Ethan—"

"Don't worry, I'll still take Rainna to the dance. But I'm starting to believe what your dad said about you three years ago. Maybe you aren't the right person to raise that little girl."

Charlie felt like she'd done a belly flop into a cold pool. She drew in a shaky breath as she heard the door to his cruiser slam shut. Malachi was standing in the doorway staring. She looked down at her empty hands. She had been so close to getting the police file. While she didn't doubt she would still get her hands on it, now there was a big question mark as to when.

Afraid he would see how rattled she was by the interaction with Ethan, she didn't look at Malachi. She didn't expect anyone from town to understand her relationship with Malachi. She herself didn't even understand it. Which was why she hadn't told anyone. His brother was in prison for killing her sister. But Malachi didn't have anything to do with that.

Ethan's reaction had been dramatic. She hadn't expected that from him. She didn't know if he was mad because she didn't believe in his investigation, if he was worried that she was being taken advantage of, or if his pride was hurt because another man was in her home.

His parting shot about her raising Rainna left her reeling. She had sacrificed the last three years of her life to Rainna and had given her love and a more stable home than anyone else. She knew that; Ethan knew that. Her gut told her he was trying to hurt her, but that didn't lessen the pain.

"Hey," Malachi's deep voice pulled her back. "I don't know what all that was about. But I can see that you're a great parent, in the pictures on these walls, the artwork on the fridge, and the way you talk about her. I didn't mean to cause trouble for you by dropping by today. I just wanted to see you. You've been so wonderful with all of this. I can't imagine anyone else would be willing to consider that the jury got it wrong. You've lost so much, but you're still willing to make sacrifices to help others. You're brave. I'm a little bit in awe of you."

Charlie cleared her throat to try and dislodge the knot that formed there. He was staring at her. The words from the students, Zack, and Ethan hung like a heavy mantle on her shoulders but tears pricked her eyes at his compliment. Without thinking, she stepped into his space, and his arms wrapped around her. "Do you want me to head out?" he whispered into her hair.

"Don't worry about it. He's caused me plenty of grief over the years, and he doesn't decide what I do with my time or who I spend it with."

Buck chose that moment to push his head in between them so hard that Charlie's foot caught on the rug, and Malachi caught her by the arm before she fell.

Charlie cracked up laughing, and Malachi joined in. They spent another hour talking about a little bit of everything but the case before Malachi left. Charlie told him about growing up with Dani, their mom dying and how that caused Charlie to start cooking, fights with her dad, and her impulsive marriage that ended when they realized they weren't the people they thought they were.

Malachi told Charlie about his parents and stories of Darius from when they were young. Malachi's interest in real estate came when his parents had their house foreclosed on when he was younger. It made him want to have the power to help people when they had housing issues. He even told her about a woman who walked out on him in the middle of a date when she found out his brother was in prison for murder. He gave her the arson report he got from the attorney and left before she had to pick up Rainna.

As she washed dishes in the kitchen, she couldn't stop herself from wondering who was right. Zack who said she didn't have the right to make others relive that night? Ethan who said she might not be the right person to raise Rainna? Or was Malachi right when he said she was brave?

CHAPTER 17

———

Rainna ran up the stairs with the speed of someone playing tag on the playground. A few minutes later, she skipped downstairs in a tutu.

"Auntie, can we practice for tomorrow's dance?"

"Of course, sweets. You know I'll never turn down a chance to dance with you."

"Hey, Rain," Charlie said while they were swaying around, "why didn't you tell me about the daddy/daughter dance?"

Rainna kept dancing, and Charlie prodded her with a hip bump, "Rainna?"

"Because you would say we don't need a man. But I want to be like my friends. They all have daddies to go with, so I wanted one too." Rainna's voice got louder as she was speaking, and her cheeks were flushed.

Charlie pushed Rainna's hair behind her ears and pulled her chin up so Rainna was looking into her eyes. "Sweets, I'm proud of you for taking things into your own hands and finding a date."

"Really?"

"Really. Now let's practice some more."

They practiced twirls, dips, and lifts until they were exhausted, and Rainna said she was ready for the dance. After Rainna passed out, Charlie went back downstairs to look at what Malachi had brought. She skimmed the first few pages of the report but was too tired to concentrate.

The next day, the house smelled like burnt sugar and every inch of the kitchen was covered in ingredients or overdone salted caramel cookies. She had been trying to put a twist on her grandmother's recipe all day, but she kept burning the caramel and overcooking the cookies. Her alarm went off and she snatched her phone from the counter.

Charlie picked Rainna up and they ate a quick snack instead of dinner, knowing Rainna would eat at the dance.

Rainna's dress was bubblegum pink with a fitted top and a tulle skirt with sparkles. It wasn't Christmas-themed, but it was what she had and loved. Rainna begged for makeup, but Charlie would only let her have lip gloss and a touch of sparkle eye shadow.

At precisely six o'clock, Ethan knocked and Rainna and Buck raced to the door.

"Hey there, princess. You look like a ray of sunshine. You ready to dance?"

"Yes, yes, yes!"

Charlie was watching Rainna's giddiness as a surge of melancholy hit her. *Dani should be here.* Dani should be the one seeing this moment. Her nose stung, and her eyes filled with moisture, but she blinked it away.

"Can I get a picture of you two on the porch before you leave?" Charlie asked.

"That sounds great." Ethan met her gaze with a look she couldn't decipher. He didn't look angry at her anymore, but she wasn't sure what she saw in his expression.

They spent the next five minutes posing for silly pictures. Some of Ethan and Rainna, a lot of Rainna by herself, and then Ethan took a few of Rainna and Charlie.

"All right, little miss. We better head out. Go grab your coat." Ethan told Rainna.

Rainna's Mary Janes tapped on the floor as she ran to grab her coat, leaving Charlie and Ethan alone on the porch. Charlie was looking at the pictures they had just taken on the phone with a small smile on her face.

"Is it alright if we talk for a few minutes when I get back? Maybe you could put Rainna to bed, and then we can chat?"

Charlie tilted her head. It didn't seem like he wanted to chastise her anymore. "Sure."

Rainna and Buck came barreling out the front door and Rainna launched herself into Charlie's legs, making Charlie almost lose her balance. Charlie picked her up and hugged her tight, inhaling the strawberry scent of the lip gloss.

"Love you, sweets. Have a great time. Make Mr. Ethan take some pictures."

"I'm on it," Ethan told her. Charlie handed over the keys to her Jeep so Ethan could take a vehicle with a car seat. They buckled her in and backed away. Charlie rubbed her arms as she made her way back inside. She grabbed some trail mix and looked around the empty house.

Her phone was still open to the photos they had taken. Rainna looked happy with Ethan.

Charlie made her way to where she had tucked the file from Malachi. She couldn't do anything right now about Rainna only having one parent, who was only an aunt. But Charlie did have an arson expert's report to dive into. She wished it was the police report so she could see if there was more information about Liam or any other possible suspects.

Even with Ethan's reassurances, something about the doctor still felt off.

Charlie snagged the report and started reading. Most of the information in the report was in the expert's testimony—from the information he was given, his opinion was that the fire was most likely an accident. He was provided evidence samples and the photos of the crime scene and he could find no indication of accelerants. While he'd identified the origination point, he couldn't say if the fire started because a candle fell over or because someone held and purposely lit something on fire.

Charlie's phone buzzed. She saw a notification for Instagram. Thinking she would look at it later, she returned her attention to the report. Her phone buzzed seven more times before she got to the end of the page. Each buzz was a new notification. She groaned and opened the app. She had thirty-seven new comments and some more likes. Thirty-seven seemed excessive. Her activity page showed that almost all the comments were from the same account but on different posts. Each one was the same.

sick_of_charli1234 commented: take ur stupid blog and leave town

Thirty comments were on Charlie's recent posts from that account—all within the last hour.

"Ugh…" Charlie rubbed her forehead and started deleting the comments and blocking the account. She dealt with at least one of these a day, but they didn't usually comment on that many posts or have insulting names and comments.

A knock came from the front door, and Charlie shuffled the papers back into the folder and made her way to open it.

Ethan was holding a sleeping Rainna over his shoulder. He looked toward the stairs in question, and she nodded. She led Ethan up the stairs and into Rainna's room. He laid Rainna on the bed and mouthed, "Downstairs," with a tilt of his head. Charlie nodded as she went to the dresser to pull out some pajamas for Rainna. She helped a very sleepy Rainna into her pajamas and kissed her goodnight.

Ethan was sitting at the bar in the kitchen, holding a cup of coffee that she had brewed earlier in the night for him. She didn't drink coffee herself, but she still had everything to do so from when her nana had lived in the house. Her grandmother had died a few months before Dani and left the house to Charlie, but Charlie didn't want to move back. The house had been vacant, and Charlie was about to list it for sale when Dani died.

"How was tonight? Thanks, by the way."

"She's so great. Honestly, it was one of the best nights I've had in a long time." He smiled sincerely and it was easy to forget she was mad at him. He had always been like that, knowing just what to say or do to make her forget that things weren't as they should be.

"I'm glad. I'm excited to hear all about it from Rain."

"I owe you an apology, Charlie." She was tracing the line of grout on the kitchen bar with her finger. He bumped his elbow against hers to pull her attention to him. When she looked up, he continued, "I'll be honest. I don't get why you're looking into this, and I have no idea why that guy was at your house. I don't trust them. I can't believe you do. But you've always looked at things a little differently than everyone else." He paused and scratched his jaw. "I'm not doing this right. What I mean to say is that I care about you. I don't want to see you hurt. I'm afraid that whatever's going on right now is going to hurt you. I know you've learned how to take a few knocks over the years, but I'm worried this one's different. I'm worried about the day you get knocked down and don't pop right back up."

She was staring at him as he slurped his coffee. His words struck a chord. What was the end of all this? Did she really think she could find the answers to what happened to her sister?

"It doesn't excuse it, but I wanted to explain. That's why I overreacted. What I said about you raising Rainna, that's not true. I was mad. I wanted to wake you up." He looked up from his coffee. She was frowning and he shook his head. "But that's not how you work. I'm sorry."

She couldn't look at him while he was talking, so she listened while running her finger over the line of grout again. She heard the rhythm of his breath beside her and the ticking of the clock in the hallway, not sure she had the words to respond yet.

"Are we okay?" he whispered, and she could hear a catch in his voice.

"Thank you for your apology," she said looking at him. "But Ethan, I need you to stop trying to decide what's best for me. Or Rainna—"

"I know. I do. I know." He grabbed a canvas bag from the floor that she hadn't noticed. "Here. Live your own life."

Her pounding heart sped up when a peek inside the bag confirmed her suspicions. He was giving her a copy of the police file.

"We both know that you would go through the process of making an official request. It's a closed case. I can't keep it from you, so there's no point in delaying you. All... all it would do is change the way you think of me," he said.

He swallowed and slowly reached out to touch her shoulder. "It's late. Thanks for the coffee and for letting me take little miss tonight."

She nodded and cleared her throat. "Thank you... thank you for this," she looked at the bag in her hands, "and for tonight."

He moved to the door and she followed him. "Ethan," he stopped and looked back at her. "It means a lot to me that you brought the report. Thanks."

Ethan shrugged. "No problem," he mumbled as he made his way into the night.

CHAPTER 18

The blinker on Charlie's Jeep clicked from a forgotten turn signal as she drove aimlessly around town in the foggy morning. She didn't want to go home. She needed to do something different. She wanted to shake off her unsettled feelings. *Is this all just going to lead me back to where I started, but with more enemies?* After starting this journey, she felt compelled to continue. She could go back home and comb through the police report that she'd briefly skimmed the night before, or she could do something more proactive.

Charlie had slept fitfully. The fear she had felt when Rainna jumped on her bed and woke her up wasn't fading. She had been dreaming about a time when her father had taken her and Dani to the movies. Charlie's mom had been sick, and her dad had taken them to get out of the house, but he had disappeared halfway through the movie. Her father always joked that if they weren't good, he was going to leave them for someone else to raise. She thought he had done exactly that. In the dream she saw her mother in the lobby, but that didn't make any sense. Charlie had forgotten all about that memory and was trying to remember what parts were real and what was a dream.

Charlie felt like she needed to keep moving and see people to get rid of the unsettled feeling following her since she woke.

The emergency room, with only a few people waiting in it, was quiet when Charlie made her way through the automatic doors. She went to the receptionist and asked for Patty and Rachel. The woman at the desk seemed a little put out that Charlie didn't have an emergency but said she would check if they were there.

Charlie saw Dani's work friends every once in a while around town, but she had never sought them out. Rachel was a few years younger than Charlie and Patty was another twenty years older. Charlie had no clue if they would be working today, but she stopped at the coffee shop on the way to the hospital and picked up drinks for them just in case.

Taking a seat in the hard plastic chairs, she watched the news on the screen in the waiting room. The couple in the corner waiting kept glancing at her and whispering to one another. After a few minutes, she heard footsteps.

"Oh my goodness, Charlie, look at you! Prettier every time I see you. How's sweet, Rainna? Do you have a picture?" Charlie stood up to greet Patty. She had known her most of her life since Patty had a daughter in the grade below Charlie. Patty's floral scent hit Charlie's nostrils as she bent down to hug her. When Charlie pulled back, she realized how much she had been avoiding moments like this the past few years. Most people in Charlie's small town loved to hug, but Charlie had closed herself off so much from everyone but a select few and had lost out on that aspect of human interaction. Charlie didn't like it when most people hugged her, but Patty's felt motherly and strong, bringing comfort.

"Hey, Patty. You doing okay? How's Heather?"

"I'm great. She's great. Just had another baby. Now let me see a picture of Rainna." Patty held her hands out, and Charlie pulled up a picture of Rainna from the monkey bars.

Patty placed a hand on her heart as she stared at the picture. "She looks so much like her. She's beautiful."

"She is, and she really does."

"What brings you by, honey?" Patty motioned to the chair that Charlie had vacated, and they sat down.

"Oh, I brought you a coffee." Charlie handed Patty the coffee. Patty waited while Charlie tried to find the words. "This is awkward. I'm not sure where to start."

"Just start at the beginning. No reason to feel awkward with me, sweetheart. After all these years around here, I've seen and heard it all."

"Well, I guess I feel like I don't know much about Dani's death. I know things like this don't always have an easy explanation, but I want to see if I can fill in the holes. You and Rachel spent more time with Dani than anyone. I talked to her a lot, but calls aren't the same as seeing people every day. Could you tell me what was going on with her in those last few days?"

"Honey, it's been a long time." She reached over and patted Charlie's hand. "Does this have anything to do with the rumor goin' round that you don't think that man did it?" Her question was direct, but her tone didn't hold any animosity. Charlie glanced around the room. No one seemed to be listening to their conversation. She nodded.

"I'm sorry it's still so tough for you. Let me think." She tapped her acrylic nails on the arm of her chair. "Let's see. She'd worked earlier that day. We were on the same shift. We had a couple of regulars come in, no real emergencies. She was a little down when we got in because one of her patients from the day before had died overnight. Stroke. Nothing we could do, but Dani always took it personally. I'm pretty sure she left here to get ready for her date. She was excited about seeing him that night. Such a shame"

Patty shook her head and stared at the ceiling like she was looking into the past. "Oh yeah! She got a call from daycare. Rainna was running a low-grade fever. She couldn't get away, so she called your dad to bring her here. She said he seemed a little put out when she called him, but he brought her by."

Charlie picked at her fingernails. "Was there anything else? Anything that seemed weird? Or even anything that seemed normal?"

Patty rubbed the pad of her index finger over her lips. "I think about that day a lot. I loved her like one of my own." Patty shook her head. "If I remember right, Dani realized Rainna's paci was missing and ran out to your dad's car to get it. When she came back, she had a funny look and said he wasn't alone, but I don't think she said anything else about it. We spent the rest of her shift getting Rainna checked out and taking turns watching her. She had an ear infection."

Charlie thought back to picking Rainna up after Dani's death. Antibiotics and an ear infection didn't ring a bell for her. Maybe Rainna got over it on her own?

"Is there anything else you can remember about that time?"

"She was mad when she left here because Dr. Sullivan pulled her aside. He said she hadn't filled out a chart right. It turned into quite the scene, as all their little tiffs did. I've always felt sorry for him that he was the one who had to be here that night. After all their history, they ended on a stupid argument. From what I hear, she was gone before the ambulance brought her in, but I'm sure he wishes he could have saved her."

Patty reached over and grabbed the top of Charlie's hand. Charlie was shaking her head trying to make sense of what Patty had just said. "Liam..." she paused and looked at Patty, her pulse speeding up. "Liam was the one who, he was..." Charlie had a hard time finding the words as a picture of her sister being wheeled into the hospital flashed in her head. "Did you say that Liam was here that night?"

Patty squeezed Charlie's hand. "Yes. I wasn't. But I've heard about it. I heard he handled himself well until he had to call it. After that..." she paused and looked toward the doors to the emergency room. "Well, you can imagine."

Charlie couldn't imagine. She didn't know Liam, but imagining what it would be like to officially say an ex was dead and there was no more hope was outside Charlie's realm. She felt like a deflated balloon. Talking about her sister's death was hard enough, but now the one guy that she wanted to dislike, her one suspect, sounded like he was busy the night Dani died. Her dislike of him was giving way to pity for the situation that he was forced into.

The automatic doors opened, and a woman came in holding a crying blonde girl who looked seven or eight. "Well, that's my cue. It's been good seeing you, darlin', but I've gotta run."

"Thanks so much for talking to me. Tell Heather I said hi." Charlie stood up and hugged Patty. More questions were bubbling to the surface at Patty's revelations, but now wasn't the time. Maybe she could ask Rachel. "One more thing. Does Rachel still work here?"

Patty was walking toward the door that was marked for staff only. "Yep, but she moved to L&D. I think she's on right now if you want to try and catch her. Bye, now." The heavy door swung shut behind Patty as she went back to work.

Without thinking too much about anything Patty said, she went down the hallway toward the labor and delivery wing of the hospital. Rainna had been born there, so Charlie knew the way. When she made it to the reception desk, she saw Rachel sitting on the desk with her back to Charlie while she chatted with the person at the desk. It must have been a slow day all around the hospital.

"Rachel," Charlie called to get her attention.

Rachel's head whipped around. "Charlie!" Rachel hopped down from the desk she was sitting on and ran over to hug her, the bun on her head bouncing with her perkiness. Charlie and Rachel had known each other in school but never hung out. After years of working with Dani and then Dani's death, Rachel had started greeting Charlie like her long-lost best friend. The receptionist gave Charlie a once over and continued typing.

"What are you up to? Rainna's not in the ER. Is she?" Rachel glanced behind Charlie like she was looking for her little shadow.

"No, no. Nothing like that." Charlie smiled and shifted her eyes to the receptionist at the desk and then back to Rachel. "Do you have a few minutes to chat?"

"Sure! I've got a mama in labor, but she's only at a two. It's her first kid, so it's gonna be a while. I can't go far, so let's sit here." Rachel pointed to a couple chairs on the other end of the waiting room. These were upholstered chairs, much more comfortable than those in the ER.

"How are you?" Charlie asked handing over the coffee that still felt warm.

Rachel looked at the coffee and smiled. "Aren't you sweet. I'm good. Busy. I've got this and I'm a nutritionist at the health club up town. I also do some personal training."

Rachel looked at Charlie from head to toe. "Not that you need it, but if you ever want a trainer, let me know."

"I will." Charlie smiled.

"So what's up with you?" Rachel asked.

"Well," she rubbed her palms on her jeans, "I'm trying to wrap my head around everything that happened with Dani. I feel like I never got the full story, and I want to know more. You were as close to Dani as anyone. Do you remember those last few days? Anything would be great."

Rachel's jaw dropped open slightly. "So it's true! I'd heard you were looking into Dani's murder and that you were hanging out with Darius's brother." Rachel looked over at the receptionist who quickly looked away when Charlie's head also turned. "What's going on there? Spill."

Charlie could feel her heartbeat accelerate and a flush of heat on her neck. *That was fast. Did Ethan say something?* Charlie desperately wanted to ask who Rachel had heard it from, but she didn't want to engage in the back and forth of gossip. Rachel would want to know about Malachi, and Charlie didn't feel like sharing.

"Rachel." Charlie gave her a hard stare.

"Fine. Be a spoilsport. You never learned how to be any fun." Rachel smirked, and then her face took on a more serious expression. "Well, I was on a shift when they brought her in. Is that what you want to know?"

Charlie cleared her throat. "I didn't know you were here. Um... wow. That must have been tough. I'll listen if you want to tell me about that or if there's anything else you can remember about the days leading up to it."

"I remember the commotion. It had been quiet that night, but when the EMTs brought her in, they brought a lot of noise with them. They knew her, of course, and they were all shook up. She was naked, but someone had thrown a robe over her bottom half. They had a CPR mask on her and were doing everything they could, but it was clear they knew it wasn't helping. The moment they hit the door, they started yelling for help. Dr. Sullivan and I ran in to help. I started to lose it, but Dr. Sullivan snapped us all out of it and into gear. He worked on her for a long time, but nothing helped. She was gone." Rachel reached up to adjust her bun, "I think that's when I decided to leave the ER. It just took a bit for an L&D position to open up."

Charlie felt a tear slide down her cheek. By keeping to herself, she'd never had these conversations. She hadn't taken the time to realize that other people missed Dani too. Rachel changed her job, Liam was there at the end, Patty made it clear that she thought about Dani all the time, and Zack had said it was one of his worst nights. Dani's death had affected people in profound ways. She put an arm around Rachel, not having words.

Finally, Rachel continued, "I remember Ethan coming by the next day to ask me a few questions. He asked me when the last time was I saw Dani alive. That was the day she died. She was getting off her shift, and I was starting mine. She was going to get ready for her date. We hadn't worked a shift together in a few days. The last time I worked with Dani, she comforted me. Brent and I had broken up again, and we spent a lot of time talking about that."

Charlie looked at the silver band on Rachel's left hand. "You two are good now?"

Rachel beamed. "Married six months yesterday."

"I'm happy for you." Charlie smiled. "Did Ethan ask you anything else?"

"He asked if I thought there was anyone who could have done this to Dani." She paused and picked at a loose string on her scrubs. "Isn't it always the boyfriend? That's what the TV shows say. She'd seen him that night, and when she was brought in, she was naked. Nobody else makes sense."

Something about Rachel's surety that it had to be Darius finally made what had been bothering Charlie click into place. It was too obvious. Everyone always looked to the significant other first. He was the last one to see her, and his DNA was on her. If he killed her, he would have to be incredibly stupid. Darius didn't seem stupid. It was easy to see how everyone else had gotten from point A to point B, but Charlie thought they were overlooking that intelligent people didn't kill others in a way that led straight to them. When she thought about it, the idea of Darius being the murderer didn't make any sense at all.

The sound of Rachel picking at her scrubs drew Charlie back. She gave herself a quick head shake. "Was that all? Did you talk to him about anything else?" Charlie asked.

"I don't think so. Oh, wait, he asked if there was anyone else Dani didn't get along with or who might hurt her. I said, of course not. Dani was great. Everybody loved her. She and Dr. Sullivan had words sometimes, but he was the only one. He never would have hurt her. And he was on the same shift as me that night."

"Thanks, Rachel. I really appreciate it. Oh, one more thing. Patty said something I was curious about. She said that on the day Dani died that Rainna had an ear infection, and Dad brought her—"

Rachel didn't hesitate. She was shaking her head, "Nope, that wasn't the day she died. That was a few days or a week before. I remember 'cause we were workin' together that day. I helped watch Rainna for a bit."

"That makes a lot more sense. Anything else happen that day?"

"Nope. We only had a couple of hours left when Dani got the call from daycare. I don't remember why she couldn't go get Rainna herself, but she called your dad. Let's see, he carried Rainna inside, but right after he left, Rainna started losin' it because she didn't have her bottle or a toy or something. Dani booked it to the parking lot. She came back a few minutes later looking out of it. I asked her what was up, but she wouldn't answer. Just said something about seeing a ghost."

Charlie shook her head. She had no clue what could have happened, but it seemed strange that both Patty and Rachel remembered parts of the incident.

"Thanks, Rachel. I'll let you get back to that first-time mama." Charlie stood up and returned Rachel's hug. "Congratulations on the wedding. Tell Brent I said hi."

"Bye, Charlie. Give me a ring if you ever want to go over to the Fort some night to dance."

"Bye." Charlie smiled to herself as she made her way out of the hospital. As much as she loved to dance in her kitchen, she wasn't the type of woman who went dancing at clubs.

Talking to Rachel had solidified it for Charlie. Darius couldn't have done it. He was the easy solution to a complex problem. Unfortunately, Charlie's list of suspects was woefully short. Maybe she would have to start looking for that ghost Rachel mentioned. But where did one find a ghost?

CHAPTER 19

———

Buck's cold nose was pressing into Charlie's hand as she sat at the table staring at the police report. Everything in the file stacked together made a pile a few inches thick. It felt too small to be the final piece of Dani's life.

There was a large stack of photos, handwritten notes, a copy of the autopsy report, death certificate, phone and banking records, and a few more things. Ethan had probably given her more than he had to.

Maybe the real killer was somewhere in these pages.

Charlie grabbed the notes. They were in chronological order, so she started with the notes from the night that Dani died. The town had few officers, and usually, only one was on duty at night. The first officer on the scene was Harvey Knight. Harvey was a few years older than Charlie but still someone she had known pretty much all her life.

The fire department and EMTs beat him there. By the time he got there, Dani had already been removed from the fire. They were in the process of leaving in the ambulance. Charlie remembered from Harvey's testimony in the trial transcript that he had pulled Darius over that night. If

Harvey pulled Darius over around 12:15 a.m., spent a few minutes with Darius, and also went to the scene, there should have only been a small window in between the two events. No more than ten minutes. Realizing Harvey had also been at the scene, Charlie understood how everyone would have believed his timeline for the night.

Darius said he had been pulled over by Harvey closer to 11:30 p.m. Darius's timeline made sense for his drive home. It was a three-hour drive and the timeline Darius gave lined up with when his home alarm was disarmed. But how would Harvey have mixed up the timing for the gap in between when he pulled Darius over and got the call for the fire at Dani's house? Darius's timeline had the gap at closer to an hour, but Harvey's timeline would be close to ten minutes. Taking the location of Darius's home from the town, Charlie looked up the mileage and then calculated how fast he would have been driving to get home on Harvey's timeline. With Darius's timeline, he would have driven an average of sixty-six miles per hour, but with Harvey's it would have been a little over one hundred miles per hour.

Charlie put her head in her hands and sighed. Something was off. Someone was lying, but who? Both had facts that should put truth on their side, but when compared with the other's testimony, neither made sense.

As she moved the documents around, a yellow Post-it came loose.

I could tell where your head was the other night at dinner, so I wanted to make sure you got your facts straight. He was at the hospital all night—charts and witnesses confirmed.—E

She shuffled the papers to see where the note had been. It looked like it had come off of the death certificate. Charlie grabbed it. Underneath Dani's personal information was the information on her death. Charlie had her own copy of the document for taking care of Dani's estate, but she had never paid attention to the details other than the birth and death dates.

The boxes checked told her that Dani was declared dead in the Emergency Room. The time of death was noted along with the fact that an autopsy would be performed. At the bottom of the certificate was the attending physician's signature. Liam Sullivan, MD had signed and attested that to the best of his knowledge, the death occurred at the time, date, and place stated.

The document confirmed what Patty and Rachel shared earlier that morning. Her sister's ex had been the one to declare her dead. It seemed incredibly unlikely Liam could have had anything to do with her death, especially after talking to Rachel. She felt a prickle of guilt for judging him so harshly. It couldn't have been easy for him to have dealt with that situation. He probably seemed cold to her because she reminded him of awful memories. Her gut told her he had been cheating on his current wife with Dani, but being a cheater didn't make him a murderer.

In the blur that surrounded Dani's death, someone had told her that Dani was unresponsive at the scene. First responders rushed her to the hospital while performing CPR. A doctor, who she now knew to be Liam, called her death shortly after she arrived because of how long she had gone without responding to any life-saving measures.

The notes from the medical examiner were under the death certificate. Two causes of death were listed. The ME listed asphyxia due to smoke inhalation as the primary cause of death and traumatic brain injury was listed as another cause.

Charlie dropped her head on the table and sighed. She had begun to wish just about anyone other than Darius had done it. His letters got to her. How could someone who wrote the things he did have killed Dani? Also, she liked Malachi, and she didn't want his brother to be a murderer.

Maybe Ethan was right. No one else seemed to be a good suspect. Maybe it had to be Darius.

A stack of photos lay underneath the death certificate and the ME's notes. She grabbed them to see if she could find a picture showing where Dani was found to visualize it. The photos weren't on photo paper, just copies of images on regular paper, but at least they were color copies. Unlike the notes, the photos did not seem to be in chronological order. There were a few autopsy photos that Charlie wasn't ready to face yet, so she kept looking. She saw some close-ups of the fire damage by the door, and then she got to a photo of several items: keys, a phone, a man's wallet, and a few other things. She pulled the photo closer to examine it and sucked in a breath. She hadn't seen it in several years, but one of the items looked eerily familiar.

She thumbed through the photos to see if she could find the item again, but that was the only picture. The image seemed to be an inventory, so she flipped through to the notes to see if she could find a log of the items. She had to go through everything a couple of times to find it. Finally, she found the inventory from when Darius was taken into custody and booked.

- car & house keys
- leather wallet, license, four credit cards, two membership cards, $100 bill
- phone, black case

- pocket watch
- pack of gum
- comb
- smart watch
- list (dry cleaning, James Kensington, groceries, wine, basketball with Isaac)

Charlie pulled the photo back to get a better look at the pocket watch. After studying the photo for several minutes, she leaned back in the chair and groaned. It felt like she had been punched in the gut. She had finally made her mind up that it didn't make sense for Darius to have killed Dani, and this one photo changed everything.

Charlie was ninety-nine percent sure the pocket watch in the photo belonged to her grandfather. It was pure gold and very valuable. A fellow soldier had given it to him in the war as a thank you after Charlie's grandfather had saved his life. It wasn't until several years later that he discovered its value. The last time it had been appraised, it was worth more than ten thousand dollars, and that had been several years ago. It was left to Dani when their grandfather died.

Charlie hadn't realized it was missing when she packed up all of Dani's things. And she didn't think the police had ever noticed that it wasn't something Darius should have had. Was this the motive? Had Darius needed money, and this was an easy way to get it? He could have taken the watch without killing Dani. Maybe it wasn't about the value of the watch. Could it have been a trophy that he took after killing Dani?

The churning in her stomach increased, and Charlie grabbed her phone before she could overthink it.

Charlie: Did you get your brother's personal items after he was booked?

Malachi: No. I thought they kept everything for evidence.

Malachi: Why?

Charlie: I need to talk to Darius.

Malachi: Okay, do I need to give him your number next time I talk to him?

Charlie: in person

Malachi: Oh. He's in gen pop, so he can have visitors on Saturdays.

Charlie: Is it too short notice to be added to his list for tomorrow?

Malachi: Wow, you're serious.

Malachi: He's had you on his approved list for years—just in case. I was planning to go see him this weekend. Is it okay if I come with you? He's only allowed one visitation with two people per week.

She hesitated. In some ways it would be nice to have a friendly face, but wouldn't he be more friendly to Darius than to her? However, she didn't want to cause him to miss a visit with his brother. After losing Dani, she couldn't imagine taking that time away from someone.

Charlie: that's up to you

Malachi: I'll make sure everything's good for you to visit

Malachi: Is there something I should know?

Charlie: We'll talk on Saturday

Charlie's sick feeling morphed into anger. The only explanation she could think of right now for Darius having the pocket watch on him was that he stole it. If he'd stolen it, him killing Dani made a lot more sense. Ethan's words about Darius letting Dani pay for her own meal came back to her. Could he have needed cash? The rest of the crime still felt like it pointed a finger right at Darius, but maybe the fire was meant to make everything look like an accident. Perhaps she was too quick to say it was too obvious.

Confronting Darius would be difficult, but no more difficult than dealing with Dani's death. Charlie was going to find out why all this had happened. Maybe it was good that Malachi would be there. It might make Darius less likely to lie to her. Or it could mean that Darius would lie just to save face in front of his brother. Either way, she was determined to get the truth, and then she wanted to be left alone.

Charlie couldn't focus on work until she made sure everything was ready for her visit to the prison. She called Winnie to see if she could watch Rainna for several hours on Saturday. Charlie went online to find out what she needed to know about prison visitation to ensure her clothes didn't break any rules and that she didn't have any prohibited items on her or do anything she shouldn't do. The prison's website said since she wasn't a family member, Darius wouldn't be allowed to make physical contact with her, which she found comforting.

Charlie tossed and turned all night until it was time to give up and get ready for the day. Even though she knew Rainna would have fun playing at Winnie's, Charlie made Rainna's favorite crepes for breakfast to make up for missing most of a Saturday with her.

When Charlie dropped Rainna off later that morning, Winnie was at the door leveling a stare at Charlie. "You will tell me what you did today when you get back. I know you're up to something. I keep hearing rumors about you, Charlie, and I'm worried. While I don't care about what they say, I don't want to be the friend in the dark. And I'm guessing you probably need someone to talk to, whether you'll admit it or not."

Charlie nodded. "Yes, ma'am." Once again, Winnie had made her feel like a wayward child. Everything was confusing enough right now. She hated that she had to justify herself to people. Even if they were people she loved, and she knew they meant well. She squared her shoulders and rolled her neck, trying to shake off the irritation. She blew a kiss at Rainna and Winnie before she headed toward the penitentiary. It was time to decide for herself if Darius was the monster the town had made him out to be, or if he was an unlucky man surrounded by a series of unfortunate coincidences.

CHAPTER 20

The prison was a massive compound, mostly brick, but it had long ago been painted white. Chain-link fences with barbed wire wrapped around the top in addition to the brick boundary walls enclosing the whole area.

Other than stories of the days when the prison rodeo drew in crowds from miles around, the only thing Charlie knew about the prison was that it was the site of a massive riot. Her nana had refused to take them to the rodeo because she remembered the riot in the early 1970s caused by overcrowding that led to hostages, deaths, fires, and significant property damage.

Pushing away those unpleasant thoughts, she pulled through the gate and found her way to the visitor lot. She spotted Malachi's black SUV and pulled her Jeep beside him. He looked up from his phone when she put it in park and killed the engine.

Malachi hopped out and came toward her while she was putting her phone and purse in her console. "Hey, have you seen this?" He placed his hand on her door and held his phone up.

She glanced up long enough to see an app and then motioned for him to move so she could get out. "My Instagram?"

"Yeah, you've got some pretty crazy comments on your latest posts. I think you should look at them." He held his phone out to her again, but she waved her hand.

"I get crazy comments from trolls all the time. Put your phone up, and let's get this over with." She patted her pockets down, making sure she didn't have anything she wasn't supposed to. When she looked up, he was staring at her with his eyebrows scrunched and his lips pursed. He tilted his head and went back to his vehicle to put his phone up.

"Hey, it's good to see you again," he said as he lightly touched her arm. Despite how angry she was at Darius and the whole situation, she couldn't keep the corners of her mouth from turning up at his smile.

"It's good to see you, too." He pulled her into a hug, and some of the tension that had grown over the course of her drive eased. She had debated with herself over whether to tell Malachi about the watch. She had decided that she wanted to see his expression when she asked Darius about it. Would he know anything? Or understand its significance?

Charlie felt dirty after checking in and being searched by a guard whose gaze lingered too long on her legs and backside and who gave Malachi a look of distaste. "You two together?" he asked, looking back and forth between Charlie and Malachi as he admitted them into the visitor's room.

Charlie pretended she didn't hear the question and turned to Malachi. "Lead the way."

Several families were already in the visiting room. The buzz of chatter grated on Charlie's already sensitive nerves. She should have realized, but she hadn't thought about other people being around when she confronted Darius. Most of the families in the room looked like they were trying to bring a big enough slice of joy to the person they were visiting to hold them over until the next visit.

It only took a few minutes of waiting at a cold, metal table, for Charlie to wish she had worn a warmer sweater. The building was drafty, and it didn't feel like the heat was on. Her leg bounced under the table and she picked at her nails until she pulled one back to the quick, causing a sharp intake of breath. Malachi bumped her knee with his, raised his eyebrows at her, and looked toward the finger she was holding. She held up her hand to show him the nail. Malachi held her hand in his and squeezed it. "You okay?" he asked.

She was shaking her head when a guard opened a door opposite the one they had entered. Darius walked in. He made his way over to where Malachi and Charlie were sitting with a shy smile. He was slightly shorter and broader than Malachi, and he didn't have a beard, but their resemblance was unmistakable. Charlie wondered if some of his breadth came from not having much to do but work out. Or maybe he worked on his muscles to seem tough to the other prisoners. He sat opposite them holding his arms stiffly at his side. Charlie realized her hand was still in Malachi's and she hurriedly pulled her it away, not wanting Darius to get the wrong impression.

"Thanks so much for coming to visit me, Charlie. I've always wanted to meet you. Dani talked so much about you that it feels like I met you years ago." His smile seemed earnest.

Charlie felt like she was wearing wool on her bare skin, and she scratched at her arm. She was here for one reason, and he thought she was here for another. On top of that, her manners were trying to take over. She almost told him she was pleased to meet him. She took a deep breath before she allowed herself to speak, "Why did you have my grandfather's watch?"

Malachi's head whipped toward her and then to Darius while Darius's eyes flashed surprise. Darius held her gaze for a moment and nodded.

"So you think I did it. That's why you're here." She heard a question in his words, even though he'd said them like a statement. A look at Malachi showed disappointment, but she was unsure to whom it was directed.

"What am I supposed to think?" Her voice cracked at the end, and she felt a surge of embarrassment. She was embarrassed she had ever questioned what the cops, a prosecutor, and the jury had agreed upon. She was embarrassed that she was sitting here, across from the man convicted of her sister's murder, and she couldn't keep the emotion out of her voice. She was embarrassed that she was drawn to his brother. But most of all, she was embarrassed because she had somehow lost herself, and she couldn't seem to get back to who she wanted to be. She was clenching her fists so tightly in her lap that she was afraid her nails would break the skin.

Nodding and looking slightly hurt, Darius continued, "I get that. I never told you I had the watch, and I'm sure it took you by surprise. Back when I was arrested, I knew having it on me looked bad. So I didn't bring attention to it. I guess because it was a man's watch, nobody realized it wasn't mine. They didn't even think to ask, which is funny now that I think about it, because I was already wearing a watch." He gave a dry laugh and rubbed a hand over his head, "But the real reason I had it? Dani had told me about the watch. She said she was sad that it hadn't done more than sit in a box since your grandfather died. She'd seen a woman wearing a necklace with a pocket watch pendant and said she wanted to do that. I found a jeweler in the city who could make it run again and turn it into the type of necklace she wanted. She gave it to me the night she died. I had an appointment to drop it off the day I got the call about Dani and drove down to speak to the police. That's why it was in my pocket."

"Do you remember the name of the jeweler?" Charlie asked, nauseated from the roller coaster of emotions she was on trying to decide if he did or didn't kill Dani.

"It was Kensington's. I talked to the owner's son." Darius scratched his chin. "I think his name was John. No! Jimmy or James. I bet they keep appointment records. Maybe you could call."

Charlie put her elbows on the table and dropped her head in her hands. *Shit.* Dani had told her about the necklace idea. His story had triggered the memory. Everything fit—even the note in inventory with James Kensington on it. She had looked at the photo and the inventory so many times in the last few hours that every detail was etched in her memory. Charlie had jumped to conclusions like a frog jumping lily pads on a pond.

She had spent close to two months slowly coming to the conclusion that Darius couldn't have done it, and with one picture, she'd thrown all that time away. Why was it always easy to believe the worst of people?

Charlie groaned and banged her head on the cold, hard metal of the table. "I'm an idiot."

Malachi cleared his throat while bumping her leg with his. She looked up to see him inclining his head toward the correctional officer watching them closely.

Oh right, not the time or the place for self-pity.

"That makes sense," Charlie said, looking up at Darius. Closing her eyes, she tried to take a quick inventory of her thoughts, deciding to continue on a more friendly note. Opening her eyes, she made eye contact with Darius, "I jumped to conclusions."

"You have every right to."

"So..." Darius looked at Charlie and Malachi and when neither spoke, he continued. "Charlie, how's the blog going? Made anything interesting lately?"

"Oh, um..." Charlie shook her head, keeping her eyes on the table as an awkward laugh escaped. How did one act after accusing someone of stealing a watch and murdering her sister? How was she going to make small talk? "Mostly just holiday stuff right now. Nothing crazy." Lifting her eyes, she saw that he was focused on her and her answer.

Malachi seemed to pick up on her unease and jumped in. "Don't let her be modest. I got to try her cooking the other day and it's fantastic. Don't tell Ma, but Charlie makes an even better scone than she does." Charlie looked up and saw them both smiling at her and a bit of the tension in her stomach eased.

Malachi caught Darius up on a deal he'd just closed. Charlie watched as they talked about Malachi's work, and then Darius shared about a new kid in prison and how he was trying to help him. The kid was having a tough time adjusting and Darius was worried he might fall in with the wrong crowd or keep himself isolated. Malachi and Darius had such an easy manner with each other that Charlie forgot her surroundings and started enjoying the pleasure of watching two people who loved each other interact. A stab of envy hit, reminding her that she no longer had that with Dani.

Charlie stayed quiet and observed Darius and their environment. Propping his elbows up on the table, the sleeve of his orange prison uniform rode up his arm. Charlie got a glimpse of a tattoo on the inside of his right bicep. It was hard to make out all the details on his skin from a glance, but the illustration looked familiar.

"What's that?" Charlie asked, pointing to the part of the tattoo she could see on his arm.

"Oh," he paused and looked down, then he lifted the sleeve on his shirt and showed Charlie the tattoo. Darius had a camel on the inside of his arm. Her heart sped up as she looked at the illustration. It wasn't a new tattoo, and it appeared to be high-quality work with intricate detail.

"Why a camel?" she asked breathlessly. Her heart was pumping as she realized the significance of his tattoo.

He smiled and looked at her. "You see, I was crazy about this woman, and for some reason, she loved camels. Kind of weird for a woman who hadn't ever seen one outside of a zoo, but who am I to judge? She had all of these crazy quotes about camels that she used to throw out to be funny. It got to be a game where I would see if I could find one she hadn't heard before." He swallowed and looked at the ceiling, his eyes bright. "When she died, I knew her memory would stay with me, but I wanted a physical reminder, too. I got this when I was out on bail. After I got convicted, I kept thinking about her and camels. Now the tattoo makes me think of one of her favorites, a Turkish proverb, 'It is easier to make a camel jump a ditch than to make a fool listen to reason.'"

Charlie's throat tightened and her eyes stung. Dani's obsession with camels was something Charlie had always made fun of. Darius had told the story with such tenderness and reverence that any lingering doubts she'd had after the pocket watch conversation had evaporated. She rested her head in her hand to hide her eyes and compose herself. A strong hand rubbed her back, and she looked at Malachi as she tried to smile without the tears spilling over.

"She told me about yours, too," Darius said, drawing her attention back to him.

"Mine?" she wasn't following him.

"Your tattoo."

Charlie took a deep breath. "She did? What did she say?" Charlie hadn't realized how hungry she was to talk about Dani.

She wanted Darius to keep talking, telling her memories of his time with one of her favorite people in the world.

"That it was your idea, but she pushed you to get it when you got divorced. That she wanted you to have a physical reminder that you were different and that you shouldn't settle."

"What is it?" Malachi touched her arm.

"A carousel."

"Why a carousel?" he asked.

"It's from a song by Kacey Musgraves, well, the inspiration for it is—'Merry Go 'Round.' It's about being unhappy but not changing. Settling." She looked down at her left hand, which still felt naked without her wedding ring, even though she hadn't worn it long. "I had once told Dani that's how our hometown felt. I always get merry go 'rounds and carousels mixed up, and carousels are prettier." She looked up and smiled with a shrug.

Baring a part of her soul to Darius around more than a dozen inmates who were having family conversations about Christmas wasn't something she had planned. She tucked her hair behind her ears and remembered the night she got the tattoo. It was before Rainna was born and Dani had driven down to celebrate Charlie's divorce being official. Dani had grabbed Charlie by the shoulders and looked into her eyes. "That guy never understood you and didn't deserve you. You got out of our town, but you settled for the first guy who asked. Don't ever settle."

Shaking her head to bring herself to the present, Charlie forgot her other reasons for coming. She used the rest of the time to get to know Darius. They talked about his routine, the books he liked, and what the food was like before she remembered his letters. "I forgot! In your letters you mentioned something in the transcript."

Darius nodded. "Right. I'm not sure it's anything. Honestly, the more I read through it, the more confused I get. I keep coming back to the arson stuff. The guy the state had swears the fire was set on purpose, but the expert we had said he thought it was accidental. I don't understand how they can have opposite views." He paused and looked around the room. "What does it even mean if the fire wasn't on purpose? Could she have fallen, hit her head and knocked over one of the candles?" He rubbed at his temples. "I mean, everything about it is so strange. There's no weapon, no injury that's from a weapon." He stopped and shook his head.

Charlie nodded. It was odd. "What about that day. What did you two talk about?"

Darius tilted his head back and closed his eyes like he was trying to see into the past. "Mostly Rainna." He smiled. "Dani was so smitten and she wanted to share everything Rainna was learning. I remember she showed me some videos of Rainna blowing kisses and climbing stairs."

Charlie smiled remembering those days of discovery. "Anything else?"

"We talked a little about work. Not much. Dani didn't want to bring us down. Your dad stopped by right after I got there. Dani met him at the door and then he left. I think she said he had left something from when he was there earlier."

"That's weird. I don't remember your testimony mentioning that," she said leaning forward.

"My lawyer didn't want it to look like I was pointing the finger at your dad. They said it would just piss people off."

Charlie grabbed a lock of hair and twirled it through her fingers. "I guess I could see that, but it's still off."

Darius shrugged. "Dani did mention that your dad was being weird, but I never thought he had anything to do with it."

"Why?" Charlie had a hard time thinking of her dad as a suspect, but it was interesting to hear that Darius didn't think her dad was involved.

"I don't know. I never really met him, but it was more the way Dani talked about him. Maybe it was because he just seemed so detached. Like he wasn't really tied to anything in the world after your mom died."

Charlie blinked, thinking about how her father had disconnected after their mother's death.

Malachi jumped in to tell Darius a story about their dad losing his phone and finding it three days later in a cereal box. Charlie tried to send her thanks to him for the subject change with her eyes. He nodded and she went back to listening.

In the middle of Darius's story about a rat in the library, the guard came to their table. They rose, and while Darius was thanking her for coming, Charlie told him he was welcome to call her any time.

On the walk out to the parking lot, Malachi bumped his shoulder against hers. "Thanks," he told her.

"For what?" she laughed. "For thinking the worst of your brother again and making an ass of myself?"

"For being willing to rethink things."

He put his arm around her shoulder, and she relaxed. Maybe her day hadn't been a waste of time, after all.

CHAPTER 21

———

"Hey, I didn't push it earlier because you seemed distracted, but I really think you should look at your Instagram." Malachi's voice was no-nonsense as they walked over the uneven gravel of the parking lot to their vehicles. Pulling her sweater tighter against the cold, she wondered why he was harping on this. He had to be familiar with internet trolls. It wasn't a big deal.

"I'll look if it'll make you feel better," she said as she opened her car door and grabbed her phone. She pulled up her app and looked at the notifications.

She had several notifications for likes and comments on her latest post. She scrolled down through the notifications skimming without seeing anything concerning when she stopped and sucked in a breath. **@death2charlie5555** had left her three comments on her latest post four hours ago.

@death2charlie5555 go back to Texas, bitch
@death2charlie5555 we don't want you and that test-tube baby in our town
@death2charlie5555 ur sister was a whore and so are you

Charlie's hands started shaking, and Malachi was there to grab her phone before she dropped it on the gravel. She noticed he had the hands of someone who did more physical labor than most who worked in an office all day. She felt her pulse quicken and she met his gaze. His arm came around her, and he pulled her into a hug. He rested his chin on her head "What can I do?"

Why did it feel like every time she took a step forward, something pulled her back? Back to indecision, back to being scared, back to not wanting to be the one to look out for others.

But she had to. Rainna depended on her, and Charlie refused to be the woman who always waited for someone else to fix things. She wouldn't let her fear show, and she would keep moving even when she was scared things were going wrong.

"This. Just this," she said as she took a tiny step and put a little distance between them. Charlie took back her phone and took screenshots of the comments. Navigating to the commenter's page, she took screenshots of all of the information there, not that there was much. It was pretty clear that this account was set up to harass her.

As much as she wanted to put this off and deal with it later, personal comments harassing her and using a threatening name were something she needed to take care of immediately. She didn't want her fans, new followers, or even writers in the space to associate her or her blog with harassment or threats.

Malachi watched her while she removed the comments and submitted a report to Instagram. Charlie let out a shaky sigh.

"I don't have plans for the rest of the day. Do you want me to come over? I hate the thought of you being alone." Malachi rubbed her shoulders. Instead of wanting to move like she had when Ethan had done it, she wanted to stay where she was and soak up the sensation.

"Ugh, I have to babysit tonight. I won't be alone," she said with a wry smile. "I made a deal with my cousin that if she watched Rainna one night while I went to dinner with Ethan, I'd watch her kids. I thought it would be during the day, but she wants to have a night in Tulsa, and then she's going shopping tomorrow. I will be the furthest thing from alone that I can imagine." Dealing with Betti's kids was a fate worse than dealing with internet trolls.

When Malachi didn't respond, she looked up at his face, "What?"

"Is Ethan the guy that came over when I was there?"

"Yep."

"You went to dinner with the guy who said those horrible things to you when I was at your house?"

"We went to dinner before you came over. I went to see if he would agree to let me see the police file."

He was still looking at her like he couldn't believe she would do such a thing when it clicked for her. "Why, Malachi, are you jealous?" She was teasing when she said it, but she immediately felt self-conscious when the words came out. She didn't want to look like she was fishing.

"No," he said a little too quickly. "Look, I don't know your history with that guy, but it seems to me that anyone who would treat you that way isn't worth your time." He reached out and lightly touched her arm, "Do you have time for lunch before you have to be back?"

"Yeah," Charlie smiled. "Lunch would be great."

* * *

Kids were running and screaming in Winnie's yard when Charlie pulled into the drive. The screen door slammed, and Winnie walked out with her apron on. "Get in here and help me with the candy. The kids can keep playing."

Charlie followed Winnie into the house and was hit by the smell of melted chocolate and peppermint. She washed her hands and took a place at one end of the counter.

"So, tell me what you were up to today. Why did you need me to watch Rainna on such short notice?" Winnie asked Charlie. Her tone was cold, and Charlie thought Winnie had guessed where she went.

"I went to meet Darius," Charlie said. Winnie had her hands on her hips and was pursing her lips. When she didn't respond, Charlie continued, "Win, what if I don't think he did it?" Charlie asked as she crushed peppermints. She took a breath and looked at her friend.

"Charlie, I'm gonna be honest." Winnie set down the spatula she was using to stir marshmallow cream. "When I heard it around town that you were hanging out with that man's brother and you hadn't told me, well, I was pissed. I didn't get what was going on with you."

Winnie was right. Charlie had kept a secret from her—a big one. While she had reasons, justifying herself wouldn't make the conversation go smoother. "Okay."

"But when I got home after finding out, I talked to Tom. He gave me something to be even madder about. I knew you had doubts. And I knew you two had been in contact with his client, but when I found out that both of you don't think Darius did it, well, that was a lot for me." She was resting both hands on the counter and looking directly at Charlie, "My husband and my best friend were keeping something like this to themselves."

Charlie nodded, not sure what she should say. When Winnie laid it out, Charlie was embarrassed. She hated the feeling of being kept in the dark. That's how Charlie felt with all the rumors she'd been hearing about Darius now that she had been looking into things. She was still disappointed that Winnie hadn't told her about the confession rumor.

"Tom told me not to be mad at you. He said I couldn't imagine what all this must be like for you. He's right; I can't." Winnie moved to where Charlie was standing and put her hand on her arm. "I'm not mad." She gave a dry laugh. "Well, I won't be for too much longer, but I still want to hear it from you." Charlie was looking at Winnie but still messing with the peppermint.

"He sent me letters. Three. The first one on the first anniversary." Charlie let out a huge exhale and felt some tension shift. "I didn't actually read them until the third one came. Something about them got to me. So, I tried to figure out what I could do. But I didn't even live here back when it happened, and it's been three years. I started with the trial transcript and some other things I had heard. Going with Tom was really the first time I looked into anything." She shook her head remembering her shattered phone screen, the joking confession, and the photo of Rainna. "And I'm sure Tom told you how awful that meeting was. Ethan gave me a copy of the police report, and I've started looking through that. But I'm lost. I don't know who killed Dani, but I'm almost positive it wasn't Darius. I'm not sure I could explain why I'm so sure, but I am."

"Wow." Winnie moved to wrap her arms around Charlie's back. "I know you aren't big on hugs unless they're on your terms, but I'm hugging you now, and there's nothing you can do about it." Charlie felt Winnie's arms squeeze her tightly, and she relaxed into the feeling of comfort, thankful for her friend.

"You're the best. You know that?" Charlie asked Winnie.

"I know," Winnie said moving back to her spot at the counter. "That's why you keep coming back for more." She winked and they both laughed.

They spent several more minutes making candy and talking. Winnie told Charlie about refusing to buy Oreos for Tom until the new year because he kept his opinion about Darius from her. Charlie shared a few of the things that had bothered her about the case: the timeline for the traffic stop, that the arson expert didn't think the fire was intentional, and that Darius being the culprit felt too easy. Winnie was so receptive in holding in her judgments that Charlie decided to tell her the story about his camel tattoo.

"You know I'm not the kind of person who'll spend her time thinking about this but—" Winnie reached over and grabbed Charlie's hand, "and I mean this—I'm glad you are. I know I told you it wasn't your job to question these things. In some ways it's not. But in some ways, it's more your place than anyone's. You deserve to go to sleep at night without wondering."

The prick of tears tickled Charlie's eyes and nose as she blinked rapidly.

"Now," Winnie said putting her hands on her hips, "I said all that, and I trust yours and Tom's opinions, but that doesn't mean I think he's innocent. At the trial, I thought he was guilty. And I know you hate it when I say this, but you really need to talk to Ethan. Whether Darius is guilty or innocent, it's important for Ethan to know the truth."

Charlie took a breath that went nowhere. It felt like Winnie punched her in the gut, giving Charlie a brief moment of validation before taking it away.

A quick glance at her watch told her she was going to be late. "I really wanna talk more about this, but I've got to go. I promised to watch Betti's kids tonight, and if I don't leave now, I won't be there when she comes to drop them off.

"Fine," Winnie walked back around to her side of the counter. "But don't think you can get out of telling me what's been going on with you and my brother lately. He's been a prickly bear, and I think it's your fault," she said as she grabbed a kitchen towel to pop Charlie as she walked out the door. She shook her head. *It always comes back to Ethan.* Then she remembered that on top of everything, she needed to let him know about the harassment on her social media.

CHAPTER 22

———

The doorbell rang while Charlie was rushing to let Buck out in the backyard and clean up the water from the bowl he knocked over. Rainna ran to get it, and Charlie's house immediately filled with the sound of boys. Betti's four boys were pushing and shoving each other and filling up the entryway. They were close in age and were competitive, vying for attention, the remote, or for glory on the ball field.

Betti followed them up the front steps and was through the doorway by the time Charlie got there.

"You've done it this time," Betti said as she tapped her yellow nails on the doorframe. She was shaking her head at Charlie as the boys made their way into the living room. They left shoes, jackets, and bags all over the floor while getting comfortable and turning on sports.

Charlie ran her hand through her hair and glanced around. *Yep, watching these kids might be the craziest thing I've ever done.* "Oh yeah? What have I done this time?"

"Where do I even start? Let's see, you've been poking your nose around the hospital. I heard you were rude to Dr. Sullivan, and now I hear that horrible man's brother has been in this house. Oh, and Sally Peters swears she'll never buy a cake from you again." Betti gestured wildly with her hands, and disapproval oozed from her.

Charlie leaned against the wall and watched Betti to see if she should be waiting for more or if it was over. "Oh, come on. Sally only bought one pie two years ago and all she did was complain about the price. What else?" Charlie asked.

"What else? What else? It's shameful. You're raising our sweet angel, and you need to get your act together. Be a grown-up, Charlie. Find a man, settle down, stop doing things to make people in this town talk about you."

Charlie fought the urge to laugh. Betti thrived on gossip. It's why she knew all of those things that she had just thrown at Charlie. It's why Charlie could never take any admonition seriously when part of the argument was to get people to stop talking about her. She tried to stay clear of Betti and her rumors; well, unless she needed to know something. They had burned her once already.

When Charlie was in high school, Ethan took her to his prom. He was a little older and on the verge of going into the military. They fell asleep in the bed of his truck looking at stars and ended up staying out all night, but that wasn't the story that made it all over town.

Charlie's dad heard the rumors, and it broke their relationship. He said he was ashamed to have her for a daughter and didn't listen when she tried to tell him it wasn't true. The rest of high school was painful, and Charlie left town after she graduated. She only came back to see her grandmother and sister.

That rumor was the reason she broke up with Ethan, too. She loved that he was steady and safe, but he didn't shut the rumor down. It wasn't a big deal to him. He said she should shake it off, but people treated her like a slut and him as a god. The stability she craved with him wasn't there anymore.

Several years later, Dani told her she thought Betti had started the rumor. Charlie didn't know the details, but she trusted Dani. By then, Charlie was married and had a new life. It no longer felt important. But it meant Charlie didn't share things with Betti that could be twisted into something else. Charlie also wondered if that's why Betti pushed her toward Ethan. Maybe she felt a little guilty.

"Betti, I don't need a man. And people are going to talk about me no matter what. I've done nothing to be ashamed of, and I don't appreciate you saying otherwise." Charlie moved toward Betti and touched her shoulder. Betti was clearly upset, and Charlie didn't want her leaving like this.

"I'm sorry, Charlie. It just gets me so riled up when I hear people talking about you. You wouldn't even believe what Katie Kennedy was saying about you when she was getting her hair done." Charlie lifted her other hand so that both were on Betti's shoulders.

"Betti, I'm not worried about what people are saying. How 'bout you try not to worry, either. Okay?" She waited until Betti nodded and squeezed her shoulders before she continued, "How's everything else?"

Betti vented for fifteen minutes about her husband making a fool of her all over town with his little bimbo. She was so worked up that she didn't even notice that Charlie was only nodding her head and not participating in the conversation. Charlie glanced over at the boys on the couch a few times because it didn't seem like an appropriate discussion, but they all seemed oblivious.

When Betti left, Charlie was exhausted, but she had a full day of dealing with house guests. Pizza was on the table and being shoveled into the mouths of five hungry kids when Buck barked and ran to the door. Ethan was standing in his uniform staring at his feet when Charlie pulled the door open.

"Hey," she said, "what's up?"

"I'm here about the report." Ethan looked like he was studying her. At her blank look, he continued, "The comments on social media."

"Oh," she slapped her palm on her forehead remembering that she had sent him a text before fixing the pizza. She wanted him to know about the harassing comments, even if he couldn't do anything about them. "Yeah, sorry. I totally forgot. Come in. Do you want pizza?" she asked, making her way back to the noisy kitchen.

Betti's kids ran up to Ethan, asking to turn on the sirens in his cruiser and if he wanted to throw the football in the backyard. They fawned over Ethan like he was a superhero. Charlie finally had to shoo them all back to the living room so she could talk to Ethan. Rainna was on Charlie's lap, but she was on the verge of passing out, so Charlie wasn't too worried about her overhearing anything.

"So, I checked what you sent me. I'm writing up a report, but it's not going anywhere. The person who made the comments doesn't have a real profile, and I'm guessing they used an email address created for this purpose. I've reached out to Instagram to see what I can get, but I wouldn't hold my breath."

Charlie nodded. He wasn't telling her anything she didn't already know. "Okay, thanks."

"Have you had anything like this happen before?" Ethan asked her.

"Well, I mean, there are always trolls on platforms like that, but it's never been anything that felt personal." Charlie thought about recent trolls on her different platforms. "Now that I'm thinking about it, I have had more weird comments on my website than normal. I deleted them, but I think I can pull them back up."

Charlie told Rainna to go play with her cousins and grabbed her computer. She pulled up the email notifications for her website. A week ago, she'd had three comments on the same day from the same person.

Anti Alan 0930—ur not wanted here
Anti Alan 0930—leave
Anti Alan 0930—i no where u live

She had thought they were a stupid prank. But now? A shiver ran down her spine, as she noticed the name of the poster and the similarity to her own last name. The numbers they used were the date of Dani's death. It couldn't be a coincidence. Could it?

Charlie forwarded everything to Ethan, and with another, "It's probably nothing. Don't expect much," he headed out.

Charlie got all five kids to brush their teeth after much cajoling and bribing. The older boys were giving Rainna a hard time about how she used to wake them up crying in the night when she stayed over as a baby. After she got all the boys settled in bed, she shut the door to the boys' room. She peeked in at Rainna, who had disappeared after brushing her teeth, and she was passed out on top of her comforter.

Charlie washed her face and opened a meditation app. She was sick of not sleeping well and had downloaded it hoping it would help. A few hours later, Charlie was trying to decide whether she should give up on sleeping and go down to look at documents when Buck got out of bed, went to her door, and started whining.

One of the boys must be up. Charlie opened her door, and Buck shot down the stairs and to the front door, where he started growling. Buck wasn't usually the type of dog to growl, and hearing it made the hairs stand up on Charlie's arms.

Charlie moved to peek through the window closest to the door. She didn't see anyone on the front porch or in the yard, but it was dark. She flipped on the porch light and looked again. She didn't see any movement outside, and she couldn't pick out anyone, but it looked like something was lying on her front mat. Maybe someone had picked an odd time to return one of her baking dishes.

Charlie opened the door and on the front mat was a piece of paper, folded in half so that it stood up like a tent. Buck went straight for it, and Charlie grabbed his collar. On the half facing the door was a message scrawled in Sharpie.

LEAVE

A cigarette lighter was next to the note. She tugged Buck back inside and slammed the door behind her. Her hands shook as she tried to get the deadbolt to line up. The bolt finally slid into place and she stepped back from the door breathing heavily.

She collapsed with her back to the front door, clasping her shaking hands. This wasn't the first time she'd been told to leave. She thought about the website comment and all the other comments on social media that seemed to want the same thing. Who was trying so hard to tell her to go?

CHAPTER 23

———

By the time the sun came up on Sunday morning, Charlie's body ached and her mind felt foggy. She had gotten no sleep the night before. After locking the door and pulling herself together, she called Ethan and then sat looking out the front window until he arrived. He photographed everything, packed it up, asked a few questions, and told her it was most likely kids. Instead of listening to her fears that the same person who was commenting online was leaving the notes, he threw her previous argument back at her. She got negative and weird comments all the time, so it was probably nothing. Why would the physical notes and the virtual notes be related?

She wanted to call Betti since the boys were in the house, but Ethan convinced her not to worry Betti. He had Harvey sit outside her house in his patrol car the rest of the night, "just to give some peace of mind." Charlie's stomach churned, and she thought it was guilt from not telling Betti immediately that something happened while Betti's kids were in the house. It felt like a betrayal.

When the boys and Rainna started to stir, she made coffee cake and omelets. Then she called Betti. By the time the call was over, Charlie was about as uncomfortable as she would be walking around with her eyebrows shaved. Betti used at least three cuss words that Charlie had never heard from her before. And while she understood Betti's mama bear instinct to protect her cubs, it wasn't like it was Charlie's fault. She had handled the situation by calling Ethan, and the house was watched by a cop the rest of the night. They were safe.

Less than an hour later, a slow knock came from the front door. Buck was lying in his bed in the living room, recuperating from playing with the kids, and barely lifted his head at the knock. Betti's husband, or soon to be ex, Mike, was on the porch looking bleary-eyed.

"Hey, Charlie. I hear you had a little trouble here last night." He smirked. Charlie pasted on a grin. She hadn't seen Mike up close in a while. Age and beer were taking their toll. A handsome young man in high school; he now had the look of someone who used to be attractive before his light hair started receding and his middle held on too tightly to the beers he tossed back.

"Mike." Charlie was tired and confused as to why he was there, so falling back onto her manners she asked, "How's the insurance business?"

Mike gave her a smile, showing all his teeth. "Great! I think we've finally got all the claims from the last hailstorm taken care of. I'm actually looking into hiring another agent."

"Oh, well, congratulations. How's your mama doing? I haven't seen her since she broke her hip."

"She's good. Starting to get around a lot better. Been giving me a hard time about Betti, of course. But you know Mom." Mike adjusted his belt and leaned against Charlie's porch railing. His mother had taught most of the kids in town piano at some point or another. Charlie hadn't lasted long. His mother was quite the taskmaster and Charlie preferred a little more freedom.

"So, what brings you here this morning?" Charlie asked. She glanced behind Mike to his maroon Tahoe, where someone sat in the passenger seat. Charlie tilted her head toward the vehicle and lifted her eyebrows in question.

Mike looked over his shoulder like he had forgotten someone else was with him. The brunette in the front seat gave a finger wave. "Do you know Traci Jefferson? I think your dad was friends with her mom. She was a few years under you in school." He gave the proud smile of a man who had deluded himself into thinking he was like Leo DiCaprio. If Charlie remembered correctly, the woman in the car was five or six years younger than her, making her about ten years younger than Mike.

"Did you hear we're getting married? As soon as we sort all this divorce crap out. Betti's been dragging her feet. She can't stand losing."

"Oh, wow. Um, congratulations." She hoped it hadn't sounded as much like a question to him as it had to her. Charlie's head was pounding from lack of sleep, and she wanted the conversation to be over. But it was hard to keep her curiosity in check. "How long have you two been together?"

Mike rubbed the stubble on his jaw, "Let's see, it's got to be about three years now, probably more, since we first started dating." He looked at the woman in the car again and smiled like a teenager. "Betti and I haven't really been living together for a long time now. I should've pushed for a divorce sooner, but I was lazy 'cause I didn't want to go through all that legal crap. It was easier to just stay with Traci and let Betti pretend all she wanted. But now that Traci and I are gettin' married, I've gotta get it done."

"Oh." Charlie shook her head, at a loss for an appropriate response.

"She sent me to get the boys. Freakin' out saying she doesn't think they're safe. Wasn't it just a note on your porch?" Charlie nodded. "Probably kids. She's always so freakin' dramatic. Thinks the world revolves around her. I guess that's why I found greener pastures," he said with a nod toward the vehicle.

"What does Traci do?" Charlie asked.

"She's a blackjack dealer. That's how we got together. I was out at the casino one night, drowning my sorrows, and I saw her. I was a goner." Mike put his hands in his pockets. "Lucky for me, she likes older men, and could see what a catch I am." He winked.

Charlie shook her head and suppressed a laugh. Mike had always been good at making fun of himself.

"Well, I guess I better get the boys and get out of your hair," he said.

Charlie stepped back so he could follow her into the house.

"Boys!" he said, his voice booming. "Grab your stuff. You're hanging out with me and Traci today!"

Charlie jumped when he yelled at the boys. She heard a couple of grumbles followed by a "Yay! Aunt Traci!"

The last door slammed after all the boys piled in the vehicle and Charlie and Rainna stood in the front doorway waving as they pulled away.

"Hey, sweets, how about we take it easy for the rest of the day? I'll let you watch whatever you want." Charlie said, tugging Rainna's ponytail.

Rainna pursed her lips as she looked up at Charlie. "How did mommy die?"

Charlie flinched like she'd been slapped. "What?"

"I wanna know how mommy died," she said crossing her arms. "You said you would tell me and you never do. She's my mommy. I'm five soon. I wanna know."

Charlie tried to catch her breath while wondering why Rainna couldn't be one of those kids who were oblivious. Instead, she'd always been this way. Questions. Noticing things. Charlie never could have imagined having a grasp of death when she was that young. But no one close to her had died until she was a little older. The three years she and Rainna had been together, Charlie had talked about Dani and that she'd died. Which meant that Rainna asked questions about when other people were going to die. It got worse when Charlie's dad died, and Rainna had two references to death in her short life.

Shutting the front door and kneeling, Charlie said, "I did promise to tell you what I know. Didn't I?" Rainna nodded and moved to sit cross-legged on the floor in front of Charlie.

Charlie sat on the floor and crossed her legs, grabbing Rainna's hand. "Somebody hurt your mommy. She got hit on the head and the house you used to live in caught fire. Somebody called 911. You've talked about that at school right?" At Rainna's nod, she continued. "But they didn't get there fast enough to save her."

"Why?" Rainna asked.

"I really don't know, baby," Charlie admitted honestly.

"But Nick said that her boyfriend got mad and hit her."

Internally, Charlie was cursing Betti's son. Now she knew what had spurred this conversation.

"Did Nick say anything else?"

"He said you don't trust the cops. But Mr. Ethan's our friend. Why don't you trust him?" Rainna asked while twirling a lock of her hair.

Treading carefully, Charlie told her, "I do trust Mr. Ethan, sweets. But sometimes people make mistakes. Do you remember when I made those brownies that tasted really bad?" Rainna nodded quickly and made a disgusted face like she could still taste them. "I cook pretty much every day, and sometimes I still make mistakes. I forget to put things in or put in too much or too little. Mistakes are really easy to make, and not just in cooking."

"Like when I put my purple shirt with your white sheets when you were doing laundry?" Rainna asked. Charlie chuckled, thinking of her almost-lavender sheets.

"Yes. Like that," she put her hands on Rainna's knees. "Sweets, no one else was there the night your mommy died. The man Mr. Ethan thinks did it, well, he seems like a nice man. I don't think he would have hurt your mommy. Not on purpose."

"So who did?"

Charlie shrugged. "I wish I knew."

"Will you figure it out?" Rainna asked, with the faith that everything in life was as simple to fix as one of her puzzles.

"I'll try." Charlie said and Rainna crawled into her lap. They sat on the floor in front of the front door for a while. Charlie played with Rainna's hair and rocked her while Rainna talked about missing her mommy. Rainna didn't want to play by herself after their talk, so they made a quick lunch and she talked Charlie into lying down with her while she napped. Charlie desperately needed sleep, but she couldn't stop her mind from spinning like a Tilt-A-Whirl at a carnival. Had Charlie shared too much or too little with Rainna? Who really killed Dani? Who was leaving the comments online? Was it the same person who left the note out front? Was the note a threat or a prank?

CHAPTER 24

———

The rusted shopping cart pulled to the left, and the cold from the refrigerated section made her tug her coat sleeve down over her cold fingers. Charlie was more rested than the day before but still felt like a mess with her oversized long sleeve t-shirt, tights, and messy bun. The note, on top of everything else, left her fidgety. She was jumping at loud noises, like the door slamming or Rainna giggling too loudly in the car. A big part of Charlie thought it was all a bad joke, but that didn't mean she wasn't still freaked out and riding the "what if?" train.

When dropping Rainna off that morning, one of the moms in the hallway at school completely ignored her. The mom was looking at Charlie and definitely heard her but refused to acknowledge her hello.

Now she was at the grocery store in town to pick up a few things for some last-minute posts she needed to get out before the holiday.

While loading her cart with eggs and cream, she ran into her teacher from kindergarten. She was retired and had to tell Charlie about all her grandkids as well as make hints about her son who was in his mid-forties but recently divorced. Charlie was finally able to shake her off after a long conversation on deviled eggs and whether vinegar, pickle juice, or Worcestershire sauce was better.

She passed a group of ladies on the baking aisle before she stopped to get more vanilla and sugar. When she turned to the next aisle, she overheard a bit of what they were saying.

"… looks horrible."

"… too thin…"

"… tacky clothes."

Pausing, she glanced down at herself and nodded. They were probably right. As she started to move on, she heard, "Spending time with the murderer's brother."

"Always was a strange girl. Thought she was too good."

"… thinks she's better than the cops and the DA. Hmph… she couldn't even finish law school."

Shaking her head, she told herself it wasn't anything she hadn't heard before. Still, it did remind her that listening in on conversations wasn't a way to boost her ego. She eased the cart away from the women and their conversation, trying to keep it from making too much noise and giving her away.

On her way back to her car after shopping while trying to keep her cart from veering into cars, she saw a familiar face. Lanie Taylor was getting out of her car when Charlie approached her.

"Lanie? I'm Charlie, I think we've met before at the playground." Charlie tried to give Lanie a genuine smile, but she was afraid that it was coming off as a grimace. At Lanie's nod, she continued, "My sister was Dani Allen. You were on the jury for her case. Right?"

Lanie nodded. She looked around like she was trying to plan her escape. Charlie felt bad, ambushing Lanie when others had most likely cornered her into uncomfortable conversations several times since her wreck.

"Are you doing okay?" Charlie asked. Lanie nodded. "I wanted to ask you about the trial, if you have a minute." Charlie smiled again, trying to look as friendly as a greeter at Disney World.

Lanie glanced at her watch and shuffled her feet. After a moment, she shrugged. "Um, okay. But I have somewhere to be, so it can't take long." Dark circles were under her eyes and Charlie noticed that Lanie was wearing a lot of makeup. Charlie eyed the parking lot to make sure no one was close enough to overhear their conversation.

"When you were a juror, what was the main reason everyone thought Darius did it?" Charlie asked. Lanie's lips pursed, and she crossed her arms.

"That's not what I thought you were going to ask," Lanie said, and Charlie stayed silent. She wanted Lanie's opinion and didn't want to make her clam up.

"He was the only option." Lanie took a deep breath and let it out loudly. "One guy said that he wouldn't be on trial if he didn't do it. Another woman pointed out that he had already admitted to being with your sister that night. His DNA was on her. What were the odds that someone else could have shown up afterward? But in the end, I think everyone saw it as a process of elimination. The defense never presented another suspect. It had to be him." Lanie kept her gaze from Charlie's. "Is that all?"

"One more thing. If that's okay," she said, knowing she had been pushing her luck from the moment she made her way to Lanie's vehicle. "What was your opinion about Darius?"

Lanie pulled her bottom lip between her teeth and squinted at the ground. After several moments, she shook her head. Charlie hadn't actually believed Lanie would give her an answer, but Lanie's refusal to say anything told her volumes. If she thought he did it, she wouldn't have hesitated to say so.

"Thanks, Lanie." Charlie reached out and lightly touched Lanie's arm. "I know I don't know you very well, but if you ever need a friend, look me up. I have experience being the outsider. I hope things get better."

Clearing her throat, Lanie said, "Thanks."

Lanie made her way into the store, and Charlie put her groceries in the Jeep while running what Lanie had said back through her head. The standard for convicting someone was "beyond a reasonable doubt," not "he's our best option." The way Lanie kept her eyes averted and her shoulders hunched made Charlie think Lanie understood that distinction.

Grabbing a few pieces of trash that had been shoved around in the Jeep while she was putting in her groceries, she opened all the doors to see if there was more. She saw a crumpled piece of paper under the front seat and pulled it free. Smoothing the wrinkles from the paper, she saw the writing.

LEAVE

It was the same message that kept popping up. Heart pounding, she glanced around the parking lot. No one was near her or paying attention. The note had been under her passenger seat. It was unlikely that someone threatening her could've left it on the inside of her car. But where had it come from then?

The carnival! Charlie remembered the note on her windshield at the carnival. She had pitched it into her car without a second thought.

With everything that had happened in the last few weeks, it seemed unlikely the note had just been someone telling her not to park there. Had someone been watching her or following her since Halloween?

CHAPTER 25

———

Papers from the police file were spread across the dining room table, and Charlie was making a list of everyone the police had talked to after Dani died.

Most were coworkers from the hospital. Family members, like her father and her. Neighbors and a few random people. Charlie had already verified that Liam and Rachel were at the hospital working that night.

The police report noted alibis. Based on the time of the crime, most people were at home. Not rock-solid alibis, even if they had a significant other to vouch for them. Charlie's dad said he was at the casino that night. Charlie scratched her forehead. *That's odd.* She'd never known her dad to gamble. She saw a note that a casino manager confirmed his story, but it didn't look like they had verified with security footage.

Charlie looked through everything else on the table to see if anything stuck out. She knew that going through everything methodically was better. However, she was still so tired and wired that she could only look for Waldo instead of a needle in the haystack of a police report.

Was the person threatening her the same person who killed Dani, or was someone playing a sick joke? She needed to get to the bottom of this. Charlie was angry, confused, a little scared, and she was done with it all.

Groaning, she pushed her chair back. Maybe she would have better luck talking to people. She slipped her shoes on, hopped in her car, and drove the short distance to where Dani's house had been. Dani had rented and the owners didn't build back after the fire. Charlie parked on the side of the road and looked around. Dani had lived at the end of a cul de sac and had three neighbors close enough to see the house.

Charlie started with the house across the street. It was owned by a couple about her parents' age. She had met them before but didn't really know them. She knocked on the door and was promptly greeted by a man in his sixties with a bushy salt and pepper mustache. "We're not interested," he said, closing the door.

"Oh, I'm not here to sell anything," Charlie told him, trying to stop him before the door shut. "I'm Charlie Allen. My sister was Dani," Charlie pointed across the street to where Dani's house had been. "Could I ask you a few questions?" Charlie smiled, hoping it was enough to get the man to give her a few minutes.

"I'm busy," he said turning to head back inside. She could hear the television in the background and assumed he wanted to get back to *The Price Is Right*.

"Please!" she said, her exhaustion sounding like desperation. "I just want to know more about what happened to my sister. Do you have a sister or a daughter?" He nodded. "Then, wouldn't you want to know as much as you could if something happened to them?" She clenched her fist to hide its shaking.

"Fine. What do you want?" he asked without moving from his position holding the door.

"What do you remember about the day she died?"

The man looked her up and down. "I've gone over all this before with the police." His voice was gruff.

"She was my sister. I want to know what happened. Did you see anything that day? Anything at all."

He studied her for a minute. "I worked that day, so I probably got home around six. Our road back here's pretty quiet, so I could hear when that boyfriend of hers got there, probably 'round seven. I go to bed early, so I didn't see or hear anything until the firetrucks got here. I think that was around three or four in the morning. I didn't go outside until the next day. By then, a ton of cars had come and gone. Trash was in my yard, and I tripped on a baseball going to get the mail. Them firemen made a mess of things, draggin' stuff out of the house, and it was blowing in the wind." Charlie looked behind her at the immaculate yard. It made sense that he was upset about trash.

"What about—"

"I don't remember anything else. Goodbye."

He slammed the door before she could thank him for his time.

She stood staring at the closed door for several minutes. Rubbing her hands over her face, she looked at the other houses and started walking to the next one.

At the second house, Charlie was greeted by a young woman with an infant. She hadn't lived in the area when Dani died and didn't know anything. When the baby spit up across the woman's chest, Charlie let her go back to her day.

As she was walking up to the third house, the one closest to Dani's, her phone buzzed.

Malachi: Hey, you okay? Any more issues on IG?
Charlie: Not on IG but IRL. Can't talk now, but I'll fill you
in later.

Charlie knocked on the door to the house. Little dogs yapped, and Charlie heard the shuffling of running feet, followed by a, "Quiet, girls!" from an elderly woman. The door creaked open, and Charlie saw Mrs. Brown, an old friend of her grandmother who couldn't be a day under eighty-five. She was more stooped than Charlie remembered and was still wearing her nightdress with a housecoat. Charlie knew from the police report and the trial transcripts that Mrs. Brown called the police when she saw smoke coming from Dani's place.

Mrs. Brown adjusted her bifocals and beamed at Charlie. "Miss Charlotte, to what do I owe the pleasure?"

Charlie leaned down and placed a quick kiss on her wrinkled cheek. "Well, now that I'm here, I realize I should have dropped by to say hello a long time ago."

Mrs. Brown waved her hand. "I know you're busy with that little spitfire. Sassy little thing as a baby. I can't imagine she's any different now."

Charlie smiled, thinking of the neon green leggings and purple oversized sweatshirt Rainna insisted on wearing that morning. "She is a spitfire."

"That sister of yours was a handful, too. Your grandmother always loved to brag. Reading at four, raising money to buy kids toys for Christmas at five, and running circles around the boys in track. Heck, having a baby with a sperm donor and a surrogate. I can't imagine anything more spitfire than that." Mrs. Brown chuckled.

Charlie tilted her head and smiled, she still felt pride that her sister was strong enough to take what she wanted from life. Dani wanted a baby, and she figured out how to have one. From the stories she remembered, Dani had read early, and she'd raised money for Christmas toys for other kids for as long as Charlie could remember. But Dani never ran track. That was Charlie.

"Dani was pretty wonderful. I'm actually here to see if you would talk to me about the night Dani died."

Mrs. Brown's face fell from elated to grave. Recovering, she waved for Charlie to come in. The house was not far from an episode of *Hoarders* and smelled of dogs and a lack of dusting. They made their way into the living room, and Mrs. Brown gestured for Charlie to sit on the pink sofa with a clear plastic slipcover. "Can I get you anything dear? I've got some cookies. You want coffee?" Charlie shook her head, but Mrs. Brown went into the kitchen anyway. After several minutes of Charlie being licked by a small dog, Mrs. Brown brought out a silver tray with packaged cookies and a cup of coffee. Charlie grabbed the cup and inhaled the scent of coffee beans but didn't take a sip. She didn't like coffee, but she didn't want to be rude.

When Mrs. Brown settled into her recliner, Charlie asked, "You were the one to call 911?"

Mrs. Brown nodded. "Yes, dear. Horrible night. Mitzy," she pointed to the smaller of the three dogs dancing around the living room, "had a tummy bug. Throwing up all night. Kept waking me. I'm a light sleeper, you see. I let her outside after she threw up, and I thought I smelled something funny. I couldn't see anything over the fence in the backyard, so I walked to the front door. A couple of lights were on at Dani's, and it looked like smoke. I called her first, but when she didn't answer, I called 911."

Mrs. Brown was staring out the front window like she could still see the night of Dani's death. Her gaze jerked back to Charlie. "You need some cookies. You're skin and bones. Always have been, but that doesn't mean I won't try to do my part to change that." She chuckled at herself and Charlie smiled. "Such a pretty smile. Like your grandmama." Charlie dutifully took a bite of the dry shortbread. She enjoyed being fussed over by Mrs. Brown.

"What else happened that day?" Charlie asked softly, trying to bring her back to the night Dani died.

"Down, Mitzy! You don't need anymore," Mrs. Brown told the dog while simultaneously slipping her a cookie. She put her index finger over her lips indicating Charlie shouldn't tell. Charlie giggled and Mrs. Brown gave Charlie a smile. "What was that, dear?"

"What else happened that day?"

"Oh, well. You know me, I was here all day." Mrs. Brown gestured around herself to the house that she hardly ever left. "Saw Dani leave that morning with that sweet baby. A few people came down our road that day. Didn't see them all. Your father stopped by and nailed one of my fence boards back for me. I heard someone on the road around when I was watching *Jeopardy.* Hmmm, that Alex Trebeck. I sure do miss him." she shook her head. "No you don't, Tootsie. You're not like Miss Charlie, here. You've got too much around the middle," she told another dog when it put its paws on the table and tried to get a cookie off the tray.

"Anything else?" Charlie asked.

"Oh, right. Well," she began. Humming under her breath, she closed her eyes for a moment and then opened them and continued, "I heard a car start a little before midnight." She tapped her lips with her index finger. "I remember the time because that was around when Mitzy woke me, and I looked at the clock. I heard another car later, and I peeked out my window. I wanted to know who was making a racket that late. I saw a big dark car like that that boy had. I went back to sleep. Of course, it didn't last long. Mitzy woke me again; that's when I let her out and smelled something. I called the police and the rest of my night was busy with that. One of the worst of my life. I'm just so thankful that Rainna wasn't there that night."

"You heard cars more than once in the middle of the night?" Charlie asked, not sure she understood correctly. The way Mrs. Brown was telling it didn't quite line up with the story in the transcript. Could Mrs. Brown have heard someone else besides Darius drive up?

"Yes." She nodded her head emphatically. "I know I heard cars more than once that night. I was up pretty much all night with Mitzy."

"But you didn't see or hear anyone?" Charlie asked, hoping Mrs. Brown had more information to share.

"No, honey, I'm sorry. Cars are pretty easy to hear. People aren't. And somebody ran over my mailbox that night. I heard that. Luckily it still worked, so your daddy put it back up for me." Mrs. Brown patted Charlie's knee like she needed comfort. Charlie thought it was Mrs. Brown's motherly instinct to comfort others, even while reliving bad memories.

Charlie remembered Darius's comment about her father coming by that night, but he made it sound like it was much earlier. Could Mrs. Brown have mixed up her times? Or had another person been by after midnight?

"You said a car like 'that boy' had. Do you mean Darius?"

"Yes, the boy that had been visiting Dani for a while."

Charlie stayed and nibbled a cookie for a few more minutes, and then she thanked Mrs. Brown for her time.

Promising to bring a pie for Christmas, she headed out. As she walked past the battered mailbox, she inspected the paint colors on the sides where it looked like it had been hit a few times, but none of the paint looked black like the vehicle Darius had driven. Who had visited Dani in the middle of the night? Was this the same story Mrs. Brown had told the police and prosecution? Could they have edited it to fit their purposes? She was a very old woman. Maybe her memory was wrong. Time had passed, and memories faded.

But if the story Mrs. Brown told her was correct, who else was at Dani's that night?

CHAPTER 26

———

A horn blared and Charlie jumped in her seat. She had been sitting at a stop sign thinking about Mrs. Brown's story and lost track of time. Checking her rearview mirror, she waved an apology as she pulled through the intersection. The car behind her was a Subaru, but the color, a brownish green, reminded her of her father's Ford Edge. Charlie didn't know much about cars and always got them mixed up. From far away or in the dark a lot of cars looked alike, especially if they were of a similar size.

Charlie's father kept coming up. Dani's coworkers had mentioned something strange with him. He was there the day Dani died, and his alibi was odd. But those things didn't mean he had anything to do with Dani's death. And if someone was threatening Charlie with the notes and comments, instead of playing a cruel prank, that person couldn't be her father.

Instead of turning right to drive home, she turned left toward the casino. Charlie couldn't imagine what she would find, but her thoughts were pulling her there.

Walking past security, she was hit by a cloud of cigarette smoke. She held her breath and took in her surroundings. It was midday on a weekday. Not too busy. But it looked like a few people were there on their lunch breaks. It wasn't a large casino, but the restaurant and gaming tables helped employ a lot of people in town.

Finally letting out the breath she was holding, she filled her lungs with the smoky air. Coming here had been rash—a mistake brought on by sleep deprivation. Charlie looked down at herself. Her hair was still messy, and she was wearing tights. While the clientele in the casino was not posh, she still felt out of place. *I'll take a quick look around and leave.*

As she walked through the room that was always bright but never from daylight, she was overwhelmed by the flashing lights and constant dings. The noise made her feel like someone was consistently winning. Charlie couldn't imagine her father in this busy environment, even as little as she knew him in his final years. He was a man who liked the simple things in life: fishing, football, and beer.

Had he lied about being here? But that didn't make sense if the manager backed him up. She must be missing something.

Charlie had almost made a loop around the building when she saw a door open to a hallway that looked like it led to offices. Charlie looked around for an employee and found a security guard.

"Excuse me. I was wondering if I could speak to the manager regarding a personal matter?" The large bald man looked annoyed but made a quick call.

"Wait here. Someone will be with you soon," he said in a deep voice after ending his call.

Charlie sat down at a nearby slot machine and examined it while she waited. She was fascinated by all the different brands and television show logos displayed on the machines. Several minutes later, a warm female voice interrupted her thoughts about the ancient queen one of the games was named after.

"Hello. I was told you wished to speak with the manager. I'm Susan Jefferson. What can I do for you?"

Charlie turned and started to stand but ended up sitting back down. She took a deep breath but couldn't feel it in her lungs. The woman in front of her looked familiar. Too familiar. She looked like Charlie's mom would have looked if she had made it to that age. She was close to sixty with long dark hair and the slightest touch of gray. She had a soft, round face and a kind smile. Charlie felt her heart race as she continued to look at the woman. She could see the differences—her mother had a small scar by her mouth, and this woman's eyebrows were thicker—but the resemblance was striking.

What bothered Charlie the most and made her palms start to sweat was what the woman was wearing. She had on a beautifully tailored navy shirt dress, a turquoise necklace, and matching earrings. It had been a long time, but Charlie would be willing to bet that the dress and jewelry this woman was wearing had belonged to her mother.

A bell went off behind Charlie, and the sound made her realize she had been staring. She shook her head quickly. "I'm sorry, I missed your name."

"Susan Jefferson. And you're Charlie." The woman smiled patiently at Charlie like she was waiting for her to catch up.

"Hello, Susan. Nice to meet you. I'm sorry, I'm feeling a little confused right now. How do you know who I am?" *Jefferson, why does that sound familiar?* "Wait, are you Traci's mother?"

"Yes, I am," Susan continued to give Charlie a kind smile. Traci's mother. Mike had said something about Traci's mom. But Charlie was too fixated on the clothes and the jewelry to remember what it was.

"Cory said you were here about a personal matter. Is this something to do with your father, dear?" Susan asked. *Mike said Traci's mom was friends with Dad.*

"Um… yes, actually. It is." Charlie didn't understand why this woman was dressed up like her mother, but her gut told her that asking her questions in the wrong way could cause her to shut down. Charlie tried to think of the best way to tread carefully.

"Well, um, I heard you were with my father the night Dani died. I just keep thinking about how messed up everything was between my dad and me. I was feeling guilty, and I wanted to talk to someone close to my dad." Charlie held her breath, hoping she wouldn't be caught in her lies.

Susan studied Charlie and seemed to come to a decision. "Why don't we go to my office?" She gestured toward the hallway Charlie had seen earlier. Charlie nodded and followed Susan. They made their way to a large office. A small sofa with a Southwestern print sat against one wall, and Susan gestured for Charlie to sit on one end while she sat at the other.

"Your father was a charming man. It broke his heart that you didn't have a better relationship." Charlie nodded, unsure where the conversation was going. "He was very sad after your mother passed. But I believe we found joy together." She looked around her office and smiled. "Don't worry. He wasn't a gambler. We met at the movies many, many years ago. I lost my husband around the same time he lost your mother, and I think we healed together."

The shock of Susan's look was wearing off, and Charlie focused on the differences between this woman and her mother. Susan's voice was deeper, her gestures less expressive. Susan continued to tell Charlie about her time with her father.

While she hadn't mentioned the number of years, it sounded like they had been together in secret since her mother died. "I was so happy when Dani found out. Your father had insisted we keep it a secret when we first got together. He didn't want you or Dani to think less of him. I think it just continued that way because that's what we got used to." Susan had a wistful look in her eyes.

"Dani knew you were together?" Charlie asked. How could Dani keep something like this a secret from her?

"Only briefly," Susan answered. "She died shortly after we met." Susan's face assumed a look of pity. "I can't imagine how hard it must be for you. First your mother, then Dani, and your father." Shaking her head, she sat back assessing Charlie.

Charlie struggled for an appropriate response while trying to ignore the grief pressing in on the paper-thin walls of her composure. "You... you met shortly before she died?" Susan nodded with a slight frown, "How did you meet?"

"At the hospital. Dani needed your father to pick up Rainna one day. I was with him and we dropped Rainna off together. I had heard such wonderful things about Dani—not just from your father. Many people thought very highly of her, and her dedication to helping others."

Susan was the ghost! Dani's coworkers had said Dani looked like she'd seen a ghost one day. She must have seen this woman and had the shock Charlie did.

Chewing her bottom lip, Charlie tried to wrap her head around everything. Nothing fit with the world as she knew it. Had her father tried to bring part of her mother back to life with this woman? And why would she be okay with it? Maybe Susan didn't know. Maybe she didn't care.

Charlie always tried to teach Rainna to think about things from the other person's perspective. Maybe Susan needed companionship and to feel valued after her own husband had died.

Charlie was lost in trying to untangle the web she had inadvertently stepped into when her phone started blaring. It was the alarm reminding her to pick up Rainna from school.

"I'm so sorry, Susan," Charlie looked down at her phone. "I have to pick up Rainna. Thank you for your time." Susan stood and walked her out.

"It was so wonderful seeing you. We should get together sometime soon. I would love to talk to you more about your father," she said.

Charlie nodded. As much as she disliked the idea of spending time with a woman who looked like her dead mother, she had plenty of questions for Susan.

CHAPTER 27

——

Buck was whining and pawing at Charlie's door. Stumbling from bed, she rubbed the sleep from her eyes. He started jumping and barking until Charlie opened the bedroom door. He ran down the stairs and to the front door growling, and she raced barefoot down the stairs after him. Charlie peeked out the window and saw smoke. Without thinking, she jerked open the door to find a paper bag on fire on her doormat. Putting her hands under the mat, she flipped it over and threw it on top of the fire, hoping to put it out by taking away the air. The rank smell hit her, and she realized the bag held dog crap.

Groaning, she called Ethan and locked herself back in the house. She banged her head on the door frame, fighting tears. This was getting old. The threats were escalating. But not to the point Charlie felt like someone was really trying to harm her. It was like someone wanted her to be scared. Flaming dog shit was a child's prank. The pranks weren't really making her question her safety, but they did make her question how welcome she was in her own hometown.

Ethan swung by and hosed off her porch. She showed him the note left on her car at the carnival, but he was still convinced someone was just having a laugh. However, he did seem more annoyed by this most recent incident. When he left, she got a few hours of sleep. In her dreams, her mother was morphing into Susan Jefferson. Then her dream turned into the dream of losing her father at the movie theater. Could that have been the night he met Susan? When her mother was still alive but sick at home?

Charlie couldn't bring herself to make breakfast, and the cereal that Rainna was eating didn't sound appealing. After dropping off Rainna, she swung by Daisy's Cafe for an infusion of calories.

She was waiting on her omelet and idly stirring her hot chocolate when she heard her name. "Charlie? Is that you?" A waitress from another section made her way over to the booth. Charlie recognized her as one of her high school classmates, Heidi Young. Heidi and Charlie had always been friendly but never really hung out. Heidi had married another of their classmates, and they had a new baby.

"Hey, Heidi," Charlie tiredly smiled up at her.

"Girl, you're looking rough," Heidi told her bluntly as she leaned down closer to whisper. "I've heard what you're doing. It seems like it's all anyone can talk about. And not in a good way." She paused and bit her lip, and then she nodded. "When I heard, it reminded me of something. When you finish, meet me out back. I'll take a break. Now ask me about the baby." Heidi straightened.

"How... how's the baby?" Charlie asked, her groggy brain trying to process what Heidi had said.

What could Heidi possibly have to tell Charlie? She'd worked at the cafe for years. Could she have heard some gossip she wanted to share?

"Great! Thanks for asking." Heidi winked. "Here, let me show you a picture." She pulled out her phone and Charlie saw a diaper-clad baby covered in what appeared to be sweet potatoes.

"Adorable," Charlie said, feeling a warm rush of emotion at seeing someone so completely happy with their life.

One of Heidi's customers waved her over and she disappeared, leaving Charlie confused but curious. Twenty-seven minutes later, with an overly full stomach, Charlie paid and walked around to the back of the restaurant. She was interested to hear what Heidi had to say so she'd tried to eat faster, but the cashier took a while to get Charlie's card back to her when she paid.

She was in a narrow alley littered with trash that was wide enough for one car to drive through at a time. No one was there when she arrived, so she kicked around cigarette butts. She would give Heidi five minutes and then head out. She probably just wanted to tell her something silly like she had seen Darius back in the day, and she didn't like him.

Charlie turned at the sound of a lighter behind her. Charlie's heart rate picked up as she remembered the lighter on her porch. She hadn't heard Heidi approach, but now she was standing in the alley with a cigarette in hand.

Heidi took a deep drag and checked whether they were alone in the alley. "You were gone awhile. Do you know who I was with before Jimmy?" Heidi asked.

Charlie shook her head. Why would Heidi ask her that?

"For a couple years, on and off, I dated Harvey Knight. You remember him. Right?" Charlie nodded, thinking about the cop who had been perched outside her house lately on Ethan's orders. "Well, he's a few years older than us and works with

Ethan now. Back when your sister died, he was the cop on duty that night."

Heidi paused, and Charlie tried to guess where this was going. The conversation seemed more significant than a piece of cafe gossip.

"Well, he was the one who pulled Darius over that night for speeding. Said Darius was a dick and acted like he wasn't doin' nothin' wrong, and he just wanted to get home. Harvey said he let him off with a warning 'cause Harvey was such a nice guy. He'd swung by the house and we were busy when the call came later that night 'bout Dani. He said he'd screwed up and let a killer get off scot-free." Heidi took another drag and nodded her greasy ponytail.

Charlie wondered if this was all that Heidi had to tell her. Her shoulders slumped and she sagged against the brick wall of the alley, but Heidi continued.

"Well, he was at the station the next day when Darius came in to answer some questions. Ethan and the other guys were busy, so Harvey pulled Darius into a side room and started in on him. Said he asked Darius why he killed her. Darius told him he didn't understand what was going on, that he wanted his lawyer. That pissed Harvey off. He told him, 'I know you did it, and you're going away forever for it.'" Heidi took another drag of her cigarette and picked at a loose thread on her jeans. "Ethan came in a few minutes later and asked to speak to Harvey outside. That's when he told Ethan that Darius told him he did it. Ethan asked if Darius had been read his rights, and he said no. When Ethan went in to see Darius, he asked for his lawyer."

Charlie's hands were shaking, and she was breathing quickly. Did Ethan believe Darius did it because Harvey told him he confessed? Had this all started because someone thought he knew the truth without investigating, so he had made up a lie?

"How... how do you know all of this?" Charlie's voice was little more than a whisper.

"He bragged about it at a party at Rhonda's one night. Well, to me, at least. I'm pretty sure a few others know, too. But not too many. 'Cause he wouldn't want Ethan to know. But he was proud of it. He said he's the reason they got that guy off the street so quick. Told me he could tell Darius was lying 'cause a his body language. Harvey thinks he's a human lie detector." She paused to shake her head. "Thought Ethan would've let the guy go until they had enough evidence, but that the confession," she used air quotes, "convinced Ethan." She tapped the ash off the end of her cigarette and took another drag.

"Why are you telling me?" Charlie and Heidi were friendly when they saw each other, but this wasn't something to tell a casual acquaintance. This was the type of thing that ruined relationships and got people fired.

"Harvey's an asshole." Heidi wrapped her right arm around her middle, clutching her left arm while still holding the cigarette. "Never hit me, but I always felt like he might. I was scared he would and that I wouldn't be able to do nothin' about it, 'cause he's a cop. When I heard you was asking 'round, I thought it might be somethin' you'd wanna know." Heidi dropped her cigarette, crushing it under her shoe.

"Break's up. I'm headin' back." Heidi turned toward the back door of the cafe and glanced back. "I'm not stupid. I know you'll tell someone, but if I'm asked about it, I'll deny it."

"Wait!" Charlie practically yelled. Something else Heidi said in passing finally clicked in place. "You were with him when he got the call about Dani?"

"He used to swing by when he was on shift and we'd have a little fun in the cruiser with the handcuffs." She lifted her eyebrows at Charlie. "Calls for house fires aren't something that happen every day. I remember that one." She turned to go back inside and the door slammed behind her.

Charlie took a deep breath and leaned against the brick wall of the cafe. If Harvey was with Heidi when he got the call about Dani, his timeline of events seemed unlikely. It was looking more and more like Darius had been telling the truth about what time he left Dani's and when he was pulled over.

The police investigation had been based on a lie. It didn't seem like they had given anyone else more than a cursory glance. Would that have been different if the police didn't think Darius had confessed at the beginning? If Harvey hadn't given them a bogus timeline?

Charlie had to figure this out. Ethan needed to know his investigation was based on a lie. Maybe she could convince him to see that zeroing in on Darius had kept him from looking at anyone else too closely.

CHAPTER 28

———

Charlie clenched her teeth as she passed the blue cinderblock walls and cubicles on the way to Ethan's office. Luckily, she didn't see Harvey. She couldn't stop thinking about the way the investigation must have happened now that she understood the missing piece about why Darius was arrested so quickly. Everyone who was part of the investigation believed Harvey's lies. They shoved all the rest of the pieces in place, even when they didn't fit.

When they saw the timeline didn't work... well, he must have driven fast.

When he didn't have a motive... well, don't all intimate partners always have a motive?

Darius never had a chance because no one would ever think anything good about him after Harvey's lie. Charlie could understand Ethan believing a guy on his force, but he still should have looked at the evidence objectively. He should have looked to see if anything disproved the theory that Darius did it rather than only looking for things that proved it. All new evidence was looked at through the lens of how it backed up Harvey's claim. Ethan should have made sure a situation like Harvey taking Darius alone into a room without being recorded never happened in the first place.

The door to Ethan's office was shut, but the window showed he was alone, so she let herself in.

"Hey, whoa. Charlie, what are you doing?" Ethan quickly rose from his chair as she shut the door behind her.

"You think Darius confessed. Don't you? That's why you're so sure it's him. That's why you never looked at anyone else." Charlie's voice was sharp.

"Charlie, why don't you sit down? You're upset. Let's talk about this." Ethan was motioning for her to take the chair, but Charlie didn't want to sit. She wanted to pace, and yell, and possibly throw things, but she decided to hold back that impulse based on her current location.

"Have you been able to get some sleep with everything that's been going on?" he asked. *Ethan had a lying cop on his force, and he wanted to talk about her sleep?*

"Answer my question," Charlie said through clenched teeth. She was sick of avoidance, and she wanted to get this over with.

"I can't comment on that." Ethan crossed his arms and looked like he was ready to face off with her. The sight of Ethan looking ready for a fight made something in her shift. Just like she didn't like being told what to do, Ethan didn't like people arguing with him. Taking a deep breath, she moved to sit in the chair. When she spoke again, it was calmer.

"What if I told you it was a lie? There was never a confession. Just someone who thought he knew the answers. Someone who didn't want anyone to get away with murder." Ethan moved back to his own chair and studied her.

"I would say that's a pretty big allegation. What proof do you have?"

She sighed and dropped her head in her hands. "None. None whatsoever. How could I possibly have any proof?" she asked lifting her head and looking in Ethan's eyes.

"Charlie, I'm starting to think you'll believe anything people are telling you. Well, except me." He broke eye contact and shook his head slowly.

Charlie nodded, feeling defeated. It was easier for him to insult her than to think he could have been wrong. "I want you to think about what you remember from the case. Your belief in the timeline and the confession rest on one person. But does anything else really line up with that? And out of those things, does anything make you think Darius would confess? Because I haven't seen anything other than him shouting his innocence." The lack of sleep and emotional toll of trying to solve the case had left her exhausted. It felt like she was losing the last piece of faith she had in someone who used to be her friend. She looked up at Ethan and could see him clenching his jaw.

"Ethan, I don't want to fight with you. But you got this one wrong. He can never get back the three years he's lost, but you can still help fix this." She pleaded with her eyes trying to make him understand how important this was.

"Charlie, I think you should go. Go home and sleep. And stop playing cop."

Charlie rose from the chair and took one last look at Ethan. His profile reminded her of a statue of an ancient Roman solider, unyielding.

"It doesn't seem like you're actually going to look into this. But in case you do. I'd rather Harvey not know that someone said he lied about these things. I don't want the person who told me to be found out."

She left, shaking her head in disgust.

An SUV was in her driveway, and Malachi was sitting on her top step. He rubbed his face and checked his watch like he had been waiting a while.

"Malachi?" she asked, confused to find him sitting on her porch in the middle of the week.

"So you're okay?" he asked with a slight smile as he stood up.

"What do you mean?" Why would he think she wasn't okay? She sharply inhaled. She'd never gotten back to him. The last thing she told him was that she was having issues in real life, and she'd get back to him, but she never did. That was yesterday afternoon.

After picking Rainna up from school yesterday, one woman who ordered holiday pies had texted to cancel. She was so passionate about not wanting anything to do with Charlie that she mentioned she would be telling everyone to stop doing business with her. After that, Charlie had plugged her phone in and left it upstairs until the front porch incident. She'd called Ethan and then put it back upstairs, where it was still plugged in.

She slapped her head with her palm. "Crap! I'm so sorry! I was avoiding my phone, and then I left it here."

Malachi cracked a smile. "I'm glad you're okay." He held out his arms, and she stepped into them. "I hope you don't think it's creepy that I drove all the way here to check on you. I just got freaked when you never got back to me and I couldn't reach you after your last message." His palm rubbed across her shoulder blades, and she sank into the feeling of someone worrying about her. It felt nice for someone to care.

"Not creepy at all." Pulling away she winked. "Come inside. I want to see how many times you stalker-called before driving three hours to check on me," she joked, feeling lighter than she had in a couple of days.

She grabbed his hand to walk inside the house. "I have so much to catch you up on. I hope you've got a little bit of time." She smiled as they made their way to the couch and she unloaded the craziness of the last couple of days.

CHAPTER 29

———

The house smelled like breakfast when Charlie got back from picking Rainna up from school that afternoon.

"Rain, I want you to meet a friend of mine. This is Malachi," Charlie said as she and Rainna walked up behind Malachi in the kitchen, flipping pancakes at the stove.

Malachi gave them a sheepish smile. "Hi, Miss Rainna. You can call me Chi. I hope you like pancakes." He bent down to her level and stage-whispered, "I don't really know how to make much else."

Rainna looked at Malachi and back at Charlie. "Is he your boyfriend?" Charlie felt a rush of heat up her neck and saw Malachi watching her and waiting for her answer.

Noticing a distinct smell coming from the stove, she laughed "Your pancake is burning." Malachi's face went from smug to worried, and he scrambled to flip the pancake.

Rainna was quiet when they first got home, watching Malachi. Charlie realized she had never really had anyone over that Rainna hadn't known her whole life. Malachi got Rainna talking by asking about movies and TV shows while they tried to eat their weight in pancakes. Rainna didn't agree with Malachi's "boy picks" for movies, but he said that *Mulan* was awesome, so she let it pass. They played Go Fish, built towers, and then he read her one of her favorite rhyming books and won her over by doing all the voices.

"Auntie," Rainna said when they were alone and Charlie was tucking her in. Malachi was hanging out downstairs.

"Yeah?"

"I... I like Chi. But I don't want you to die like mommy did."

Charlie had to catch herself to keep from falling off Rainna's bed.

"Why... what makes you say that, sweets?" Rainna was picking at her cuticles.

"Well, everybody says mommy's boyfriend killed her. I don't want you to have a boyfriend if he's going to kill you. I don't want to be all alone." Rainna's voice sounded small and she had tears streaming down her cheeks.

Swallowing past the lump in her throat, Charlie pulled Rainna to her and hugged her tightly. Smoothing her hand over Rainna's head, she gave her a kiss. "I'm sorry, Rain. I hate that your mommy isn't here with you. But don't worry. You're stuck with me."

Snuggling close, Charlie's heart ached for Rainna. She had dealt with so much loss, confusion, and uncertainty in her short time on Earth. Charlie did her best to explain that, while a few boyfriends may hurt their girlfriends, it's rare. And she also made sure Rainna knew that Malachi wasn't her boyfriend but her friend.

When Rainna was asleep, Charlie pulled out her notes and files. She wanted to figure this out. Maybe Malachi's fresh eyes could help.

Earlier in the day, she had caught Malachi up on the threats as well as everything with her dad and his secret girlfriend. His alibi was fishy now that she knew who the casino manager was. While they were setting up a low-profile security camera that he brought, they tried to figure out if her dad had somehow killed Dani. And, if so, how they would ever figure it out since he was now dead as well.

Charlie wanted to deny that her dad was capable of killing someone, but she couldn't. After her mom died, his temper had been out of control. He threw a plate of food across the room at her one night because she put too much chili powder in it. And it wasn't just her. Dani told her that when she told him that she was going to have a baby via sperm donor, he left her house in such a hurry he ran over three of her potted plants. He would eventually come around and would usually apologize, but his initial burst of anger went off like a rocket.

Charlie also vented about the lying cop and Ethan being too stubborn to listen to reason.

They were flipping through notes and pictures when Malachi asked, "So what's the story with you and that guy, Ethan?"

Charlie hesitated. She hated the story, but she was sure Malachi could handle her high school drama with everything he'd been through. She told him about the rumor that had ruined her relationships with her dad and Ethan and how it all worked out for the best as much as she'd hated it at the time. She admitted she probably would have settled for Ethan and the town a long time ago if not for the rumor.

"So, your cousin started a rumor that ruined your reputation? That's harsh."

"I don't think she meant to." Charlie paused, trying to remember Betti back then. "I think she just likes the attention."

"Hmm..." He turned back to the papers he was flipping through. "Doesn't seem like someone I'd want to be around. Any chance she did it?" he asked.

"Nope, she was watching Rainna that night. She was at home with Rainna, her husband and her four kids," Charlie said reaching for a stack of papers.

"Could it be random? Like someone broke in to steal something, she scared them, they killed her, and ran," Malachi asked.

Charlie pulled out her hair band and ran a hand through her hair. She shrugged. "It's definitely possible. I guess anything's possible. I'm not sure if anything was missing, but then again, I didn't even notice the watch was gone until I saw the picture."

They continued looking through the piles of papers.

"Okay, this is going to sound crazy. But what if we're not actually looking for someone? What if it was all an accident? Like the defense's theory at the trial."

Charlie leaned forward and put her head in her hands as she thought about it. "Do you think that could be an option?" She rubbed her forehead. "I mean, maybe the fire was an accident, but what about the head injury?"

"Don't people get accidental head injuries all the time? I hate to say it, but I'm starting to think it has to be something like that. Your notes here say she had volunteered at a blood drive. Maybe she gave blood and passed out?" Pausing, he shook his head. "Either your dad did it because he didn't want anyone to know his creepy little secret—and he's dead, so proving it's a bitch—or it was all a horrible accident." Malachi cradled his head in his hands. "Darius is going to be in prison forever," he groaned.

Charlie had never heard Malachi worked up before now. He sounded close to breaking. She'd seen first-hand the love he had for Darius, and her chest ached when she thought they may not figure this out. Thinking that Malachi's brother might be lost to him, similar to how Dani was lost to Charlie was horrifying. Darius might not be dead, but his future was bleak if they couldn't get him out.

"I'll figure this out. We're going to get him out." Charlie told him. She didn't know how she would do it, but she was determined. Her dad seemed like the best suspect, but that didn't mean it was a dead end. Maybe she could talk to Susan again. Or look through the boxes of her dad's things. When he died, she paid someone to box everything up and she hadn't looked at anything.

She searched through the papers until she found the transcript of the coroner's testimony. He told the jury that in his opinion, she had been left to die, or the killer thought she was dead. Smoke inhalation killed her. She had a severe head injury. Based on his experience, the coroner said the head injury was from Dani being shoved into something by a strong person or being hit in the back of the head with an object. Because her body was moved and the firefighters damaged the crime scene, the exact cause of the head injury couldn't be determined.

Charlie rubbed at her eyes. The pages were starting to get blurry because she was so tired.

"Maybe your accident theory's not that crazy, after all," Charlie told him. "The coroner essentially says he doesn't know how she got the head injury."

"Hey," Malachi said when he looked over and caught her yawning, "you're beat. When's the last time you really got any real sleep?"

Shrugging, she yawned again. Malachi laughed and stood up. "I'm going to head out."

"You want the spare bedroom?" He'd driven all this way to check on her and she didn't want him driving back this late. She tried not to think about the significance of him sleeping in her house. It felt big, like their relationship was changing, but she was too tired to process it and she knew offering it was the right thing to do.

"Thank you, but no. See you soon?" He hugged her and gave her a light peck on the forehead. She nodded and they walked to the front door.

Charlie felt a buzz in her back pocket as she opened the front door. Ethan was standing under the porch light. Her eyes flicked to the recently installed camera. She had set up the camera so that she would get a notification on her phone when someone was at the door. *The notifications must be working.*

Ethan's eyes went to Malachi and stopped. Charlie saw his rigid posture as he took in Malachi's hand on her shoulder. The hand at Ethan's side was opening and closing. She waited for him to say why he was there and when he didn't, she asked, "Ethan, why are you here so late?"

Ethan's attention snapped to Charlie. "Can we talk?" Glancing at Malachi he said, "Alone."

"Sure, let's go in the kitchen." Ethan walked inside and Charlie looked to Malachi.

"Do you want me to stay?" he asked, his gaze focused on the path Ethan took. Charlie shook her head. "Call me later, Charlie. I've got time. Long drive and all." Smiling, she gave him a quick hug and headed into the kitchen.

Ethan turned to her and shoved his hands in his pockets. "You were right."

Charlie ran her hand over her head, trying to figure out what he was talking about. The last few days had caught up with her, and the only thing she could think of was sleep.

"Harvey lied. I got him to admit it after a few beers tonight. Don't worry. I didn't share anything that could get back to you or whoever told you. We were talking about the investigation. I told him how happy I was that we got the guy off the street so quick and how, no matter what, he's stuck there now." Ethan glanced to where Malachi had been and shifted uncomfortably. "I'll have to fire him in the morning. I think he really thought he was doing the right thing."

Charlie swallowed. This was big. Maybe not for Darius, but for Ethan. "Do you think what he did was right?" Charlie asked.

"Lying is never the right thing," Ethan told her.

Charlie nodded, not knowing precisely what he meant, but glad to know he didn't approve of Harvey's actions.

"What I told Harvey tonight about being happy we got the guy off the street so quickly, well, that was how I felt back then. It wasn't a lie. But I don't want to be that guy who doesn't take the time to do things the right way. Look, I don't think it's going to change anything, but I'm going to look back into the investigation." He ran a hand over his head. "It'll be in my spare time because he was locked away fair and square, but I want you to know that I respect what you're doing, and I'll take a look."

Charlie was glad he was finally taking her seriously. It reminded her a little of who he was when they were younger. "I'm glad to hear it, Ethan. Now, I'm tired, and I would like to go to sleep."

Charlie walked to the front door, not checking to make sure Ethan followed her.

"Charlie, I know you want answers. That's what I'll get you."

"I appreciate that. I really do." Ethan walked out and she shut the door behind him, locking it.

Just because Ethan was finally listening didn't mean she would stop looking but finding out what really happened to Dani would have to wait until tomorrow.

CHAPTER 30

——

Charlie was humming under her breath and enjoying the sizzle of the bacon in the skillet as she finished cooking breakfast. A good night's rest, and the world seemed less bleak. She still didn't know how she would get Darius out of prison, but in the light of day, it felt possible in a way it hadn't the night before. If Harvey could be exposed for the liar he was, Darius could be proven innocent.

"Auntie, when's Chi gonna come back?" Rainna asked, coming into the kitchen and snagging a piece of bacon Charlie had set to cool.

Charlie smiled. "Did you have fun with him last night?"

"Yeah, but he's really bad at Go Fish."

"Maybe you're just really good." Charlie winked and Rainna laughed.

Charlie dropped Rainna off at school and came back to work on a post about holiday cakes in jars for unique homemade gifts. Dancing to her nineties playlist, she was enjoying the feeling of being productive. It had been a while since she'd been able to focus on the fun and creativity of her work. After she finished, she pulled the files back out for another look. The notes that had been left for her on her mat and windshield were at the top of the pile. Shaking her head, she set them aside, still confused by the strange messages.

Glancing through everything, she made sure she was familiar with all the pieces. She laid them in piles across the table based on what each section was—notes from the scene, coroner information, photos, etc. Then, she stood on the chair and looked down at everything together. The messiness of the handwriting on the police notes drew her attention and she grabbed that pile. As she read back through the events of that night, it felt like she was missing something. Most of the officers with notes in the file had horrible handwriting, but one set of notes was in all caps, making it easier to read. Looking at the notes in caps, she decided that they must belong to Harvey because they were the notes from the perspective of being first on the scene.

EMTS IN PROCESS OF LEAVING WHEN I ARRIVED...

Rubbing her forehead, Charlie tried to pinpoint what was bothering her. Something felt familiar, but she couldn't place it. She went back to reading when her phone buzzed. Buck's nails clicked on the floor as he made his way to the front door and let out a bark. Standing up and lifting her arms overhead in a stretch, she made her way to the other side of the table where she had left her phone. As she reached for the phone, she saw the note that was left on her windshield.

LEAVE

She snatched the note and made her way back to where she had been sitting. Placing the note next to the officer's report from the scene, she looked back and forth. *No... it couldn't be.*

The horizontal line on the "L" went past the vertical line to the left, almost like an upside down "T." It was not something she had seen before, other than in the police notes. She looked back and forth between the *"LEAVE"* and *"LEAVING"* she took a shaky breath.

Shit, shit, shit.

An officer had been threatening her for two months and she had just gotten him fired. While she was glad he wouldn't be in a position of authority anymore, it didn't feel reassuring now.

Buck was barking at the front door, but she could only hear the blood rushing in her ears.

She kept looking to make sure she hadn't made a mistake, but her eyes and her gut told her the same person had written both. Her phone buzzed again, reminding her that she had forgotten to check it earlier.

A notification from her new security camera was on top of a new text message.

Unknown Number: Come outside, bitch

Looking at the camera notification, she confirmed her suspicion. Harvey Knight was waiting for her on the front porch. She chewed on her bottom lip while she took a screenshot of the camera view and sent it to Ethan. She thought about waiting for him, but she didn't want Harvey to think she couldn't fight her own battles. Closing her eyes and taking a steadying breath, she opened the front door. Buck stood beside her growling.

Harvey was leaning against the railing, throwing daggers with his eyes. "Took you long enough." He glanced at Buck and then back to Charlie.

Her heart was pounding in her chest and a trickle of fear ran down her back. "Harvey."

"You've just always gotta be better. Don't you?" Shaking his head, he stepped closer to her. "I remember one time, when you were younger, you got my brother suspended from school. Did you know that? You told the principal that bathroom out by the tech building smelled funky. She checked out all the guys with tech classes and found a joint on my brother. You never could leave well enough alone."

Charlie fought the urge to back away. He was right. She had gotten his brother suspended, but it wasn't on purpose. She didn't know what pot smelled like back then, and she just wanted the principal to know the bathroom smelled bad. But she didn't think her argument of ignorance would help her in her current situation, so she stayed silent.

"You're too stupid to see it, but the guy who killed your sister is in prison. No one else could have done it. What the hell does it matter if a couple of facts are a little off?" he asked, taking another step closer. The gap between them was now only one large step. Buck growled but didn't move.

"The way things happen matter," she said, ashamed of the tremor she heard. Pushing her shoulders back, she stood a little taller. She would not let this bully intimidate her. "You didn't want someone to find out about your lies, so you tried to scare me off. Is that it?"

"The way things happen don't matter, and you're a naive bitch if you're stupid enough to think they do. Bad guys should be in prison. Doesn't matter how they get there." He reached out and wrapped his hand around her upper arm.

The shock of his painful grip on her arm almost made her lose her courage. "Did you really think comments online were going to keep me from trying to find out who killed my sister?" Buck was barking, but Harvey ignored him.

"You know who killed your sister, and he's sitting in a prison cell. I wanted you to know you weren't wanted here. And I wanted to tell you that on the place you spend the most time—your precious blog. And if you lost fans in the process, all the better." He was leaning close and she could smell alcohol on his breath. It was still early in the day. After Ethan had fired him, Harvey must've had a little liquid courage and then come to her house.

"What do you want from me, Harvey?" she asked. His being there was probably an impulse and she didn't think he had thought out his next steps.

He brought his face down to her ear and whispered, "I want you to know that nobody wants you here. I want you to leave this town and never come back. And I want you to remember this feeling, right now. Think you're better than other people all you want, but *know* that I have the power." Letting go of her arm, he shoved her into the door frame, her spine hitting hard and making her lose her balance. The moment he let her go, Buck jumped at Harvey and bit his hand. Charlie scrambled to her feet.

"Stupid mutt," Harvey lifted his foot to kick Buck and Charlie shoved him away from her dog. He fell down the steps to her front porch and was cussing as he got to his feet. He started to come back up the steps when Charlie heard a familiar voice with an edge colder than she had ever heard.

"Harvey… my, my. What are you doing here? I'll have to tell my brother that I saw you today."

Winnie was holding a paper grocery bag in one hand and her other hand was on her hip. Harvey walked past Winnie holding the hand Buck bit. "You okay?" she asked, making her way to Charlie.

Charlie nodded. Feeling her eyes sting, she reached out and pulled Winnie into a hug.

"Well, this is unexpected," Winnie said but hugged her tightly.

"Thanks for always being there when I need you," Charlie said, dashing her hand across her eyes.

"Always. But it looked like you two had it on your own," she said looking at Buck. "Oh, court was out today so I thought I'd bring over the specialty items you asked me to pick up." Winnie held out the bag of groceries with Charlie's harder-to-find ingredients. Winnie had gone shopping out of town a few days before and Charlie had asked her to swing by a specialty grocery store for her.

"You're the best," Charlie said, meaning it.

"I know." Winnie gave a small smile and then lifted her eyebrows and tilted her head to the direction in which Harvey had left. "I know you hate it when I say this, but we need to call Ethan."

Grabbing the bag, Charlie glanced down. Would she have a bruise from where his fingers dug into her arm?

"Let's go inside. I'll tell you about the asshole who's been threatening me—online and with a lighter on my doorstep." Winnie sucked in a loud breath. "Unfortunately, I don't think he's responsible for Dani's death. Too bad because I would love to see what inmates would do to a former cop like him." Charlie let out a dry laugh. "Ethan should be here any minute, actually. I texted him when I saw Harvey outside." She would make sure Harvey paid for his sins.

CHAPTER 31

───

Rainna and Charlie were walking hand in hand into the school. Rainna's class was having a party that day and she was skipping in anticipation. Looking down and smiling at the joy on display, Charlie saw a twisted leather bracelet on Rainna's wrist that she hadn't seen before.

"Hey, Rain, where'd you get that?" Charlie reached down and touched the bracelet. It looked like a necklace that she had looped a few extra times onto her wrist.

"Oh, um, this... well, I've had it," she told Charlie.

Charlie thought about it. "No, you haven't, sweets. Where did you get it?" It didn't look valuable, but Charlie still didn't like Rainna to have something she didn't know the origins of. Could Rainna be stealing?

"Nick," she said referring to one of Betti's sons. "He didn't like it. But I did, so he gave it to me." Rainna told her in a small voice, looking down at her scuffed shoes.

"Why didn't you just tell me that instead of lying?" Charlie asked.

"I don't know. Just 'cause. Sorry, it's just a little lie."

"Rain, lying is a big deal. Between the truth and a lie, lying is never the right thing." When the phrase came out of her mouth, Charlie recognized Ethan's words about Harvey. Something about the phrase was scratching at her memory, but she couldn't quite place it.

Charlie was still repeating the phrase to herself as she exited the school when she passed a mom in an SUV. The mom and the car seemed familiar. It was like they were reminding Charlie of something that was just out of grasp in the same way the phrase was. As the car pulled past her, she saw the paint was scraped off on the fender like the driver had sideswiped something. That's when it hit her, "Lying is never the right thing!" Charlie yelled to herself. She felt jittery. Had she just figured something out?

Pulling out her phone, she called Winnie from the Jeep.

"Please don't tell me you have someone else threatening you this morning. I don't have time to save you," Winnie said.

"Okay, this is going to be really random," Charlie said.

"I've been your friend a long time. I can do random."

"Do you remember at the funeral when we snuck out to the parking lot to get some air?"

"After we overheard George say he was hoping the trial would make national news?" Winnie asked, the disgust in her voice unmistakable.

"Yes. We were sitting down on the ground with our backs to your car so no one would see. Do you remember the car parked next to us?"

"The one with the awful scratch down the side?" At Charlie's affirmative sound, Winnie continued. "How could I forget? That's how we kept ourselves busy—guessing how the scratch got there. I still think they hit the sign at the McDonald's drive thru."

"Win, do you remember whose car that was?" Charlie asked, her heart pounding.

"Of course! So do you." Winnie said. Winnie confirmed the owner of the car and hopped off the call to finish her morning routine.

Charlie drove into town, barely pausing at the stop signs. She turned off Main Street and parked on a side road. She looked at the clock on the dash, hoping the back door was unlocked and that no customers had arrived yet.

Charlie tested the back door to the beauty shop and breathed a sigh of relief when it opened. Checking her phone, she opened the camera app. She started recording video and put the phone back in her pocket. She didn't hear any chatter as she made her way into the shop.

"Charlie! What are you doing here? Come to see if I could fit you in for a mani, I hope," Betti said from across the room where she was organizing nail polish. Charlie shook her head. The last time Betti had talked to Charlie, she was furious that Charlie had somehow endangered Betti's kids. Now, Betti acted as if everything was normal. Nothing felt normal to Charlie. Betti looked at Charlie's nails. "Yep. You need me. Girl, you're too old to treat your nails like this."

"Hey, Betti. Do you have a minute?" Charlie debated sitting down. She felt awkward standing, so she took the chair.

"Sure, sure. I don't have my first appointment until 9:30, I'm just here 'cause it's easier coming right after I drop the kids off. Are you here to tell me what that ruckus at your house was all about?" Betti took the seat across from Charlie and pushed a small bouquet of daisies to the edge of the table. She propped her hand on her chin like she was ready for an infusion of gossip. "You can't imagine how scared I was when you called me. I know I probably overreacted, but all five of my babies were in that house, and you said someone threatened you." Betti placed her hand over her heart like she was a Southern debutante from the eighteen hundreds who might faint at any minute.

Charlie didn't miss that Betti had included Rainna in her count of babies.

"Actually, I wanted to talk to you about something else," Charlie said.

"Well, okay. But I still expect you to fill me in on all of that," Betti said, pushing her hair out of her face.

"So, I've thought about the best way to say this," Charlie said. "I could lie and pretend I know something I don't, but that's not really *my* style." Charlie felt her heart race. She was taking a huge chance, and if she was wrong, she would never hear the end of it.

Betti let out a nervous giggle. "Charlie, I have no clue what you're talkin' about."

"Okay, so I have this theory. And it's just a theory right now, but I'm pretty sure I could get information to back it up if I needed to."

Betti's knee was bouncing, and she had a puzzled expression on her face. "Are you going to tell me what's going on? Or am I gonna have to guess?"

"You know I've been looking into Dani's case. Right?" Charlie paused long enough for Betti to nod her head. "Well, the more I look, the more I think there's no way Darius did it. I'm not sure anyone murdered Dani." Charlie had a hard time keeping still, but she wanted to get through this, and she had to pretend she was calm.

"What… what do you mean no one murdered her? That's doesn't even make sense. She's dead, and her house was set on fire. Of course, someone killed her." Betti was working the side of her bottom lip in between her teeth.

"But what if they didn't? What if it was an accident?" Betti started to interrupt, and Charlie held up her hand. "Hear me out. What if Darius came over but left when he said he did? What if they lit candles for their date night but hadn't blown them all out yet?" Charlie felt the sweat across her neck and down her back. Her sweater was too warm. She was talking faster than she wanted to, and she tried to slow herself down.

"What if someone else came over that night? Someone who had a dark SUV that looked enough like Darius's vehicle at night that someone with bad eyesight wouldn't notice the difference?"

Betti's eyes were wide, and Charlie couldn't decide if she looked confused or scared. "Charlie, what are you talking about? You haven't been sleeping good. Have you? I think you need to get some sleep. Things are gonna make a lot more sense in the morning." Betti rose to put a hand on Charlie, and Charlie shook her head to stop her.

"Betti, like I said before, I don't have proof. But..." she paused and gave Betti a stern look. "I think I could get it. I think you went to Dani's that night. I'm not sure why, but I think you did. I think something happened, and Dani got hurt. I think you hit a mailbox on your way out with the car that you don't drive anymore—but Mike does. It left some paint behind and the owner never replaced it. Your paint's still on the mailbox."

CHAPTER 32

———

Betti was sitting in her chair, shaking her head with her eyes closed.

"Betti?" When she didn't respond, Charlie continued, "Betti, I think it was an accident. I don't think you meant for any of this to happen." Charlie didn't really know, but she hoped it was an accident. She hoped no one had meant to kill Dani, especially Betti.

"You need to get out of here right now, Charlie, before you ruin everything that's between us. I can't believe you would think something like that of me." Betti sounded angry, but she had a wobble in her voice.

Charlie rose from her chair. "I wish you would tell me why you did this. I came here today because I don't think you're dangerous. I don't think you did anything on purpose. I wanted to give you a chance to tell your story—without other people speculating. But if you don't tell me, I'm not going to stay quiet and drop it. I'm going to tell Ethan my theory, and I'll keep looking into it. I'll tell Darius's attorney, and they'll probably hire a PI. Dirty secrets don't stay hidden forever, Betti."

"Why are you doing this?" Betti stood up to face Charlie. "Why are you trying to ruin my life? You've always got everything. You had the boyfriend everyone wanted, you got the brains, and now you got the baby without any of the work. But you can't be happy with what you have. Can you? You've got to ruin everyone else's lives."

"Betti, I'm not doing this with you. A man is in prison. Someone who seems like a pretty good guy. Rotting away for a crime he had nothing to do with. Don't you feel bad about that?" Charlie asked.

Betti's hands were shaking. "Why are you so convinced I did it?"

There was no nice way to say it. "Because you lie. You always have. Big lies. Little lies. You let other people take the fall for the messes you create." Charlie ran a hand through her hair. "I'm not sure you even mean to do it part of the time. I almost wonder if it's become a habit. Are you just lying to others, or do you lie to yourself, too?"

"I am *not* a *liar*," Betti said crossing her arms.

"Oh really?" Charlie's eyes got cold and she gestured widely with her arms. "Darius sells prescription drugs. Who told you that one, or did it start with you? Or the rumor about me and Ethan in high school, who started that one? What about you and Mike? He said he hasn't really been living there in years and he's been with Traci for more than three years. I'm betting that's where he was the night Dani died."

"What?" Betti looked around the shop. "What are you talking about? My husband hasn't been with that hussy for three years."

"Yes, he has. And you know it." Charlie crossed her arms.

"Even if he was, I was home with all the kids, including Rainna." Betti crossed her arms, looking triumphant that her alibi hadn't disappeared.

"Were you?" Charlie asked. "It was the middle of the night. The kids wouldn't know if you were asleep. But they would know if Rainna was crying enough to wake them up and you didn't go get her."

Shock flashed across Betti's face. "Charlie, wait! You can't do this!" A tear had slipped out and was sliding down Betti's cheek, and she was still shaking her head.

"It's not too late. I think it was an accident, and I'm sure the DA would see that."

Betti's shoulders slumped and she collapsed back into a chair. "I would lose everything," Betti whispered.

"You wouldn't. I would make sure you don't." Charlie reached out and touched Betti's shoulder talking softly. "But if you don't come clean, I will do everything I can to find the evidence that you did this. Darius doesn't deserve to sit in prison."

"He doesn't have a family that relies on him. I do," Betti argued. "The jury found him guilty!"

"They were wrong. I know it, and you know it."

Betti slipped from the chair and onto the floor, tears streaming down her face. "I didn't mean for it to happen."

"What, Betti?"

"I didn't mean for Dani to die." Betti's voice was no more than a whisper.

Charlie made her way over to Betti and sat on the floor beside her. Putting her arm around Betti, she tried to make her feel less alone. "What happened?"

"She told me earlier that day that Darius wasn't staying the night, so I went over after I thought he'd be gone. Having Rainna with me that night had been so wonderful. I always wanted a little girl. I thought that since Rainna didn't have two parents, Dani could share custody with me. I'd done all the work to get her here, anyway. No one else had to put up with swollen ankles, a restricted diet, constant heartburn, and contractions." She said rubbing her chest like she could still feel the heartburn.

"I let myself in with my key. She had just got out of the shower. I scared her because she didn't hear me come in," Betti said, her eyes shining. "When I tried to talk to her about sharing custody with Rainna, she told me to go home to Mike. But that was part of the reason I was there. Mike was out with Traci. I knew Mike had wanted a little girl, and he'd been disappointed when the last two were boys. Maybe if we could have Rainna with us, he'd want to stay. And if he didn't, at least I'd have something to look forward to."

"But Dani blew me off. When I told her Mike wasn't home, she was furious. Yelling that I'd left *her* baby alone, she said *her* baby, like Rainna wasn't even mine. I carried her for nine months. It's not easy bringing life into this world and I did it. *Me*. She's more mine than Dani's." Betti was sniffling and wiping at her splotchy red face.

"What happened next?"

"She said she was going to pick up Rainna. She didn't want me watching her again until I pulled myself together. She was overreacting. I tried to stop her. I grabbed her arm. I guess I grabbed her harder than I thought. She fell against the bathroom counter and hit her head. I tried to move her, but I couldn't get her very far. She was bleeding. And no matter what I did, she wouldn't wake up. I got scared and left. I was even more freaked when I hit the mailbox. It was so loud." Betti cradled her head in her hands. "By the time I got home, I ended up turning right back around." Betti's hair was a curtain keeping Charlie from seeing her face. "I was gonna take her to the hospital. I promise. But I saw the flashing lights, and I left."

"What about the fire?" Charlie asked.

"I really don't know. Maybe that really was Darius," Betti said, but it sounded like a question.

"Betti, you know that Darius had nothing to do with this. He was gone when you got there, and he didn't come back."

A look Charlie couldn't identify crossed Betti's face. Betti sat up and moved away from Charlie, straightening her hair, wiping under her eyes, and trying to put herself back together. "I know nothing of the sort. I don't know that he didn't have something to do with the fire." Charlie felt like Betti had erected a brick wall between them.

"Betti, don't be ridiculous."

"Ridiculous. I'm not the ridiculous one. You are. Everyone will think you are if you try to convince anyone that I had something to do with it. You're the one who thinks she's too good for this town but is still here. You're the stuck up one who won't even date the most eligible bachelor around. You couldn't keep a husband, you couldn't cut it in law school, all you do is bake and pretend like you're something special. The quitter, the dropout, the snob. You're nothing special and no one around here will ever believe you." Betti's hands were on her hips. Her confidence had returned and she looked sure of herself, "Darius was convicted, and that's what everyone believes. As far as I'm concerned, that's the truth." Betti stood up and dusted off her pants.

"Betti, what are you doing?" Charlie had been so close to fixing this and now everything was slipping away. "You admitted that you were there when she hit her head. Why are you backtracking?" Charlie moved closer to Betti, but Betti stepped behind a table to put more distance between them. Charlie's gaze fell to the bouquet of daisies and another piece of the puzzle slid into place. Betti was the one leaving flowers on Dani's grave.

"I'm not losing my kids! You can't prove anything, and you don't want to try. No one will believe you over me." Betti crossed her arms and looked like she was preparing for battle.

"This isn't about me versus you. This is about that fact my *sister* is dead. Rainna has to grow up without a *mother*. And you had something to do with it. For once in your life, own your actions."

The bell over the front door jingled and the wind slammed the door closed. Ethan was standing in the doorway.

"Betti. Charlie." he nodded to each of them. Charlie looked to see if he had heard their conversation, but she couldn't read him.

"Ethan, what are you doing here?" Betti greeted him like nothing was out of the ordinary. He was just a friend who had dropped in unexpectedly to say hello.

Ethan looked at Charlie. "I was on my way to your house when I saw your Jeep parked here. I needed to talk to you about Harvey. He was released this morning. The DA doesn't want to press charges," he said.

Charlie felt a churning in her stomach. She couldn't deal with Harvey right now. This conversation with Betti was more important. Looking at Betti, she tried to will her to change her mind.

"Betti, please?" Charlie asked.

"Mind your own damn business," Betti said.

Charlie nodded, making up her mind. "Betti was there that night. She's the reason Dani fell and hit her head. She said it was an accident. It wasn't Darius. You can't let him take the fall for this, Ethan."

"Now, Ethan." Betti took a step closer to him. "You know Charlie. Always looking for drama. Doesn't like the world the way it is, so she makes stuff up."

Ethan was silent while his attention went from Betti to Charlie and back. "Betti, let's head over to the station and we can talk about whatever's going on here." Ethan ran his hand through his hair, and Charlie noticed dark circles under his eyes. He looked like a man approaching middle age, rather than the teenage boy from her memory she usually saw when she looked at him.

"What? I don't… I mean. You know Charlie's just a troublemaker, Ethan." Betti's mouth was opening and shutting as if, for once, she didn't know what story to tell.

"Now, Betti—" Ethan said but Charlie cut him off.

"I'll send this to you, Ethan, in case she's not ready to repeat it yet." Sounding resigned, she pulled her phone from her pocket and hit the red button ending her recording. She didn't know if the recording captured everything Betti said, but it was worth it to make Betti think so.

Ethan chuckled and shook his head, "Should have known…"

Betti got red in the face. "You recorded me? Without my permission! How could you?"

"It's over, Betti," Charlie told her.

Charlie turned to leave. "Charlie," Ethan said, "I'll need you to come by the station today." Nodding, she walked out the back door, leaving Ethan to take care of Betti.

She leaned against the outside of the building, listening to the hum of traffic. It was over. She'd figured it out, but instead of celebrating, all she wanted to do was crawl in bed and cry. She missed her sister and finding out who was responsible for her death didn't bring her back.

Driving to the cemetery, she was able to keep it together. But the moment she sat on the cold hard ground next to Dani's headstone, she lost it. Having a project had helped to mask her grief for a short while, but the moment Betti confessed, it all came flooding back.

Thinking about how much she missed Dani made her remember someone else who was also missing their sibling. She pulled out her phone and made a call.

"Good morning, Charlie."

Charlie smiled at the deep warm voice that was becoming familiar and special to her.

"Hey." Charlie paused and cleared her throat to get rid of the lingering ache to cry. Thinking about sharing her news with Darius brought a sense of lightness mixed with a touch of worry for the future of Betti and her kids. "I think you need to call Darius's lawyer. I'm going to send you a file. It's time for Darius to go home.

"Wait, what are you talking about?"

Lying on her back on the cold ground in the cemetery, Charlie told Malachi about the mailbox and the SUV, Betti's boys talking about Rainna crying in the night one time when she stayed over as a baby and no one getting her, and Mike being with his girlfriend at the time Dani died. How all of the lies just kept adding up, and Charlie's gut had told her Betti was hiding something.

Charlie sighed. "I confronted Betti this morning. She denied it and I pushed until finally she confessed. She immediately backtracked, but I recorded it." A small smile touched her lips. If it hadn't been for the security camera that recorded her conversation with Harvey, she never would have thought of recording her interaction with Betti.

"Call the lawyer and make them get him out now. If every-thing goes smoothly, he'll spend this Christmas at home." Charlie could hear the smile in her voice.

"Betti. Wow." He paused. "I want to make sure I heard you right. You think with what you found, Darius can finally come home?"

"Yep. I do." She knew how much Malachi loved Darius. And while she'd never get her sister back, she loved getting to be the one to give him the gift of his brother back.

EPILOGUE

Rainna's legs were flecked with mud, and Buck's paws were caked when they came tumbling in the front door.

"Sweets, you're a mess! Don't you two dare track that through my house. Meet me around back, and I'll get the hose."

Charlie looked up from Rainna and Buck when she heard the front door creak open again. "I take it this is your fault?" she asked a sheepish-looking Malachi.

"Don't blame Chi, Auntie. Well... I mean, he did tell us that we needed to get some energy out, so maybe you can blame him after all." Rainna laughed, tugged on Buck's collar, and headed back outside. She was glad she hadn't changed into her dress yet. Cleaning Buck and Rainna was going to get her dirty.

"You always bring trouble when you come over." Charlie winked at Malachi as she headed to the back, but he grabbed her arm and pulled her into a hug, kissing her temple. Malachi lived a few minutes down the road, but he was at their place almost as much as he was at his own.

After a short visit with Winnie and some of Rainna's friends, Charlie and Rainna had driven back to Dallas earlier in the day. After everything with Betti and Darius, Charlie realized how much she had upended her life to make others happy. She talked to Rainna, and they decided to move to Dallas, but Charlie had promised they would visit their hometown often. Rainna wasn't ready to leave all her friends for a place she didn't know, but she was willing to try something new.

A handful of people in her hometown still gave Charlie the cold shoulder or hot insults to her face, but Charlie was finally starting to feel better there, too. Winnie had reminded Charlie of all the people who helped her when she was looking for answers. And Charlie was pretty sure Winnie had done some reminding to others that Charlie wasn't an enemy; that uncovering what actually happened in a murder case was a good thing.

Rainna had started school in Dallas that fall and had already made several new friends. It took a while, but Charlie finally sold her nana's place. Now their townhouse in Dallas was filled with a mix of furniture that reminded Charlie of her old life and her new one. Moving back to Dallas had allowed Charlie to collaborate with some grocery stores and set up more book launch events when her cookbook had published a few months ago. She had lived in Dallas for several years after dropping out of law school, and enjoyed rekindling her old connections.

Thirty minutes later, Rainna and Charlie were cleaned up and heading down the tollway with Malachi. They pulled into a strip mall that had recently been refurbished on one end. A food truck was out front and a bounce house was in the parking lot along with streamers and a banner pronouncing a "Grand Opening" for Darius's new project. When he'd gotten out of prison, he wanted to do something to help people who got out of prison stay out of prison. One of the biggest hurdles was finding good employment. While Darius admitted that his organization would probably evolve, for now it was focused on job placement for former inmates. He had been working for months putting together training programs, lining up employers, and finding mentors.

A man in dark jeans and a button-down shirt saw their car and waved. Once the vehicle was parked, Rainna grabbed Charlie's hand and pulled her across the parking lot. "Uncle D, Uncle D! Auntie said I'm supposed to tell you Happy Anniversary, but I don't really know why. Do you have cake? This is a party, right, so you have to have cake. That's Auntie's rule." Darius had quickly become one of Rainna's favorite people after he was released. He had lots of stories about her mom she hadn't heard, and she thought his camel tattoo was the "coolest." Darius's warm laugh surrounded them as he scooped Rainna up.

"Don't worry, sweets, I brought the cake." Charlie put a hand on Rainna's arm. "I didn't tell you because I didn't want you to sneak any before we got here."

"Cake!" Rainna wiggled and Darius sat her down. She started bouncing on the balls of her feet while Malachi and Charlie hugged Darius.

"So how do you think turnout's going to be?" Malachi asked Darius.

Darius shrugged. "Pretty good, I hope. I've been knocking on doors in the neighborhood for a few weeks now, and the profile in the paper and on morning TV should help."

Darius stuck his hands in his pockets. "Guess who called me today?"

"Who?" Malachi asked.

"Ethan. Called to apologize again. Wanted to see how everything was going one year out." Darius tugged on the sleeve of his shirt. "He also wanted to give me an update on Harvey. While Harvey may not have got any real punishment for what he did to me, or you, Charlie, at least he's paying for some of his sins now. He got caught on a security camera at a hotel hitting his girlfriend."

"Wow," Charlie said, playing with her necklace. She had taken her grandfather's watch and made a necklace for herself, like Dani had wanted to do. "I hate that for whoever she was, but I'm not sad he'll be locked up." She let out a shaky breath. When the DA decided not to do anything about Harvey assaulting Charlie, Ethan strongly recommended that Harvey leave town. Harvey had moved away, but Charlie still had nights where she jerked awake, thinking about the lighter on her porch and him grabbing her arm.

"I got an interesting call myself today," Charlie said.

"She called you today?" Malachi asked.

Charlie bit her lip and nodded. "It's part of her therapy."

"I still can't believe she never spent a day in jail," Malachi said with a touch of anger in his voice. George Marshall, the county District Attorney had chosen not to pursue homicide charges against Betti because the head injury was an accident and they never figured out how the fire started. Charlie's best guess was that Betti knocked over a candle in her hurry to escape after Dani fell. George and Betti's attorney came to an agreement and she pled guilty to an assault charge. Other than some mandatory counseling, her only real punishment was a fine.

Darius shook his head at Malachi. "Today's a good day. Let's focus on that." He bumped Malachi's arm, "Hey, why don't you two take Miss Rainna to the bounce house before it fills up," Darius told them, looking around and assessing the crowd.

Darius didn't like for them to talk about Betti or what her lies had meant for him. Even after she confessed, getting him out of jail had been a nightmare and had taken a few months. Darius's lawyer filed a writ of habeas corpus and an appeal bond, trying to get him out before the holiday. But the judge said that it was in the best interest of the community to not release a convicted murderer on bond. Then, he delayed reviewing the writ to get Darius out for good. The District Attorney didn't want to admit he had been wrong with the case. He opposed the writ that Darius's lawyer submitted, saying the jury system was put in place for a reason and the state should be able to rely on the judgment of the jury.

There wasn't anything Charlie could do about the judge, but when she found out that George was opposing the writ, she fought back. As a family member of the victim in the crime, she let George know that she was disgusted with his idea of justice. When he wouldn't budge, she told him that she would post Betti's confession online, using her 650,000 followers to get the word out. George said some pretty nasty things but, in the end, he didn't want her publicly sharing a recording that proved what a poor job he had done on the case. He dropped his opposition and joined the defense attorney in asking for Darius's release.

When the parking lot had filled up with people milling about, Darius stepped on a small platform next to a speaker and grabbed a microphone.

"Hey, everyone. Thanks so much for coming tonight to our grand opening party. For those of you who don't know me, I'm Darius Thomas, and I spent more than three years in prison for a murder I didn't commit. Today marks one year since I was released."

The crowd erupted in applause and wolf whistles. "While I was in prison, I met some really great people, who had ended up there because they didn't get the right opportunities or have the right people believing in them. I got a second chance because I had people who believed in me. I want to be that person for others. So if you, or someone you know, is looking for a job and you're someone who needs a second chance, come see me. People are more than the worst thing they've ever done. I know that and I want to help others see that, too. Alright, everyone, now it's time to eat some food, meet some people, and dance."

The crowd applauded, and Darius hopped off the platform. Music blared through the speaker. Rainna made her way to snag the first dance with Darius, and Malachi interlaced his fingers with Charlie's and tugged her onto the makeshift dance floor. She laughed, and they made their way to Darius and Rainna, all dancing and laughing together.

ACKNOWLEDGMENTS

In the last year I've been blown away by how much of a group activity it is to write a book. I've been blessed with a phenomenal community who helped make this dream of mine possible.

Nate, thank you for being my rock and my cheerleader—for giving me pep talks when I needed them and ridiculous suggestions for the book when I needed a laugh. You're the best. Also, thank you for finally reading a book. I'm so happy it was mine.

J, O, & M, thank you for inspiring me every day.

Thank you to the wonderful individuals who read the messy early drafts and gave invaluable feedback. You helped me see the pieces that were missing and the many ways in which my words could be interpreted. Susan Ray, Leigh Camp, Cherish Gehret, Becky McGee, Jen Welsh, Denise Hale, Laura Croteau, and Brittany Wilson, you're amazing and I'm grateful.

Jay Ray, thank you for connecting me with Eric Koester and the Creator Institute. Thank you for immediately believing I could write a novel. And thank you for telling everyone that I was writing a book, even when I wasn't ready for you to. The accountability was invaluable.

Mark Smith, thank you giving me a job that introduced me to the world of actual innocence and wrongful convictions and allowed me to learn from experts in the field.

Chauntelle Wood, thank you for pointing me in the right direction when I had a question.

Naomi Howard, thank you for talking me through my questions on appellate law.

Jen Welsh, Melissa O'Neil, and Brittany Wilson, thank you for the weekly Zooms filled with support. I needed every single one of them.

Thank you to the Creator Institute and New Degree Press for the community you've created to give writers the tools they need to tell their stories. Thank you Eric Koester, Haley Newlin, and Kyra Dawkins for sharing your wisdom. Thank you, Cassandra Stirling, for helping me discover the story I wanted to tell as well as helping me gain the confidence to do so. And thank you Bianca Myrtil for helping me to refine the story.

Thank you to all the innocence projects out there for the amazing work that you do.

Last, but not least, I would like to thank the wonderful community of people who supported me in my pre-sale campaign and helped to make this dream a reality. I wish I could describe how amazing your support makes me feel. This book wouldn't be possible without you.

Alan L. Adams

Amy Adams Brewer

Erich Almonte

Whitney Anderson Llamas

Anthony Arguijo

Jennifer Atzenhoffer

Lisa Baker

Robin Banell

Cassie Bates

Victoria Bishop

Nathan Box

Melinda Brinlee

Laura Brown

Rachel Butler

Eric & Karla Camp

Mindy Carter

Linda Chanow

Justin Clapper

Brittani Clemmons

Adam Cocke

Jason Conley

Martise Cooks

Kevin Corcoran

Taylor Crosby

Laura Croteau

Stacy Crowe

Jessica Dark

Cynthia Delgado Matlock

Chanel Dobrzenski

Emily Donnellan

Kendall Doughty

Katie Duke

Shannon Duncan

Patrick Dunn

Jamie Edwards

Debra & Stephen Enis

Tod Everage

Abi Fain

Denis Fallon

Lacey Foster

Howard Frankenfield

Ryan Frome-Pezzulli

Amanda Gamble

Cherish Gehret

Dana Gilbert

Lizet Gomez-Lluguin

Jessica Gore

Anna V. Gryska

Eric Gudmundson

Amanda Hale

Denise Hale

Casey Hansen

Luke Hayes

Kenneth Hedge

Isaac Henry

Kara Herrnstein

Mauri Hinterlong

Miles Indest

Amanda James

Jayshree Jewett

Kristin Jurica

Bri Keller

Erin Kessler

Benedict Kirchner

Courtney Klimcak

Bradley C. Knapp

Jessica Knight-Long

Daina Knoblock

Jennifer Koehler

Eric Koester

Natalia Kolakowska

Adam Kowis

Alexander Kuiper

Tyler Lambert

Lee Langdon

Louie Layrisson

Cally Lee

Lucas Liben

Peter Loudis

Amanda Lowe

Kae Lu

Eduardo Marquez

Jillian M. Marullo

Crys Masterson

Tyler McClain

Kacey McConnell

Lorryn McGarry

Becky McGee

Lauren McGee

Brett Miller

Malori Mills

Luis Miranda

Cynthia Mitchell

Adam Morgan

Melissa Munson

Tamara Nash

Sarah Nealis Bohan

Tina Nguyen

Ashley Nguyen

Laura Olive

Melissa Kerwin O'Neil

Joe Ope

Kelly Ormsby

Liam O'Rourke

Tade Oyewunmi

Tiffany Palmer

Kelly Perrier

Dalton Perse

Jason Phillips

Brett Podkanowicz

Roy Prather III

Diana S. Prulhiere

Kelly Ransom

Jay E. Ray

Michael Razeeq
Jayme Reynolds
Tracey Rice
Laura Robertson
Jordyn Robinson
Rachel Scarafia
Krystal Scott
Meredith Scott-Kaliki
Alexander Sementelli
Sarah Sheldon
Steven & Kat Smith
Freddy Sourgens
Lauren Vargas
Elly Vecchio

Allison Walker
Julie Walker
Kenyon Weaver
Andrea Weide
Jerrell Welch
Jen Welsh
Missy Westfall
Malory Wiest
Brittany Wilson
David Winn
Robert Woods
Pam Yother
Jared Young
Joshua Zaccardo

Made in the USA
Coppell, TX
30 June 2022

79426024R00162